COMPUTE!

COMPUTE!

How? Where? Why?
Do You Really Need To?

Brian J. Ford

HAMISH HAMILTON   LONDON

First published in Great Britain 1985
by Hamish Hamilton Ltd
Garden House 57-59 Long Acre London WC2E 9JZ

Copyright © 1985 by Brian J. Ford

British Library Cataloguing in Publication Data
Ford, Brian J.
   Compute! : why? when? how? do I need to?
   1. Electronic digital computers
   I. Title
   001.64   QA76.5
   ISBN 0-241-11490-X

Filmset by Pioneer
Printed and bound in Great Britain by
Richard Clay (The Chaucer Press) Ltd, Bungay, Suffolk

Contents

Introduction

'*The vogue for home computers is a con.*' The chances are you do not need one. The current craze is a phenomenon like the miniskirt, the hula-hoop and the skateboard, and it will fade into obscurity as dusty micros retreat into attics and to the cupboard under the stairs.

There is no shortage of books which will expound the wonders of a computer and relate, in high-flown terms, how they can be operated. In my view there is a vital question we must address before we reach that euphoric state: how great is your need for a home computer?

The faddishness of the computer era assumes that everybody who does not own one will fall by the wayside as progress trundles on. I do not believe that for an instant. Most of the computers that have been bought for home use have never been programmed by their purchasers, and when they are used it is usually to run software that comes ready-made. Even here, though, the *use* which most home micros have is surprisingly small.

Do not assume from this that computers themselves are overrated in the technical sense. They are astonishingly compact, effective and inexpensive devices (p. 5) which perform tasks which a few years ago would have seemed unimaginable (though there is nothing mystical about that, p. 105). If you *do* use a computer to solve a problem then you will be amazed at its speed and its accuracy. But there are important doubts about the accuracy of commercial software, which is often littered with bugs and is surprisingly illiterate. The failure rates of home computers are higher than one would hope, too.

The element of the 'con', however, lies in the way that computers are marketed as easy-to-use necessities. They are often neither of these! A second theme is that you are taught to believe that a knowledge of computer programming is a vital part of preparing for life in the immediate future. This is also untrue. You do not need to master computerology in order to interact with the benefits computers convey, any more than you require training in photochemistry to take snapshots at the weekend.

Here, then, is an introduction to the computer world. It sets out to explain the essential terms of the trade, to account for the development and the state of the art, and to help you come to grips with the uses to which you might be able to put a micro in your own life. It does *not* assume that you necessarily need one — but it does assume that, even if you decide against it, you will know something of the way the new era is heading, and what it means.

Meanwhile, if you conclude that you do need a micro, then I trust it will be for informed and genuine reasons. The marvellous applications of computers to transport booking terminals and bank cashpoints will convince anyone of the uses which we already take for granted. Yet, at the same time, we should also bear in mind the confusion presented by many computerised accounts and statements and the interminable delay which many information banks inflict on customers, ever since they introduced a computer in Head Office; which reminds us that machines, unless they are wisely and sensibly used, can create more problems than they solve.

So: confidence trick or marketing reality? Thorn in the side or personal panacea? Unintelligible nonsense or technical necessity? Read on, and if some of the dilemmas in your mind can be resolved by this book, I shall be delighted. And if computers become rather less forbidding, and the world they inhabit more familiar in the process, then I will be greatly relieved.

Brian J Ford
London, 1985

1 Power-up!*

What can a home computer do best?

You could almost offer a prize for the best answer to this question. We have become obsessed by the miraculous tasks computers can perform. But a computer cannot do *anything* on its own. All a computer does is speed up complex tasks of information sorting and retrieval. How successful it is depends on three things:

1. The information must be of a useable kind. This means that the data the machine is given must be sensible.
2. The sorting procedure must be of the right kind. This means the machine must be programmed correctly and well.
3. The right use must be made of the results. This is related to the common sense and experience of the people who apply the results.

A computer can do things no person can, it is true. This mystical ability is equally true of a chisel, a pencil or a typewriter.

But the question is a fair one, all the same. Here is your micro-computer, gleaming on the table. For what will it be most valuable? Calculating? Doing homework? Integrating lifestyle variables into meaningful situations? Abolishing your overdraft? None of these, I fear, is the answer.

The best task a computer can undertake at home is playing games.

Games?

Games? Is that all?

Well, no — there *are* many clerical chores that you could systematise with a computer and they can be used to facilitate many tasks which involve the filing and retrieval of information, (to keep your mortgage record, your bank balance, lists of addresses, family blood groups even) but some of these tasks can be done more rapidly with a pen and paper, and the calculations they involve are often still best performed on the back of an envelope.

The best job for your micro-computer is electronic game-playing, without a

---

*This is jargon, though standard throughout the industry and not to be confused with the jargon discussed on p. 88. 'Powering-up' is what ordinary people call switching on a machine.

doubt. Gobbling up the enemy, bombing him, zapping him from aircraft or spaceships, escaping from tunnels in which you leave him trapped and buried alive. . . . There is no end to the gory possibilities embodied in the modern computer game. The fact that the might of modern technology at its most advanced (i.e. solid-state physics as encapsulated in miniaturised computer systems) is most widely used to train young people into simulated extermination of their fellow-humans need not concern us here.

But one thing must be said right at the start. *Many of the purposes for which we are advised to use micro-computers are simply dreamed up by faddist enthusiasts who have been borne along on a wave of novelty, excitement and the prospect of profit.* These people will use a computer to do anything under the sun that involves the sorting of information. The only problem is that in the majority of instances the time taken in putting the information INTO the computer is out of all proportion to the value of the process you eventually get OUT . Of course, there are many interesting tasks that computers can carry out, and some of them we will return to. However, the essential question of what they do *best* is easily answered: they play games.

Could a computer run my home?

Another very fair question. Certainly you would find it possible to develop a program that would run the dish-washer, feed the dog, serve a perfectly-boiled egg. Many articles have insisted that this would be the immediate future facing us all.

But the amount of equipment you would need to do this in practice would be costly and complex, and people often buy apparatus that they find troublesome to use *in practice* no matter how attractive it appeared to be *in theory*. There are homes cluttered with gadgetry which seemed so useful in the store, but which pale into irrelevance when seen in the more down-to-earth perspectives of a domestic environment.

The trouble with much of the thinking about labour-saving and automation is that it seeks to give an illusory impression of the future, as though it were the sole function of electronics to take over the business of living. Television has already shown how easy it is to cast off normal societal functions in order to devote great segments of daily living to watching a screen. The point about many of the activities which occur in our homes is that they provide a useful and enjoyable means of creating an environment, and in many cases they are a catalyst for family contact.

If I had to support a future domestic use for computers, it would be for the carrying-out of deeply monotonous tasks, like vacuuming the floor. A carpet cleaner is usually moved around the same area by the hand that uses it, and this kind of monotonous task can easily be memorised by a micro-computer and then repeated on command thereafter. In that form of application a computer has much to offer. But if children have to lose out on the fun of

2

bath-time, with a caring parent upstairs twiddling the taps, then heaven help tomorrow. I feel much the same about the driverless transport systems which follow signal-generating coils embedded in the roadway. What happens there to the passenger who drops her purse, who wants information, who is being hassled by a noisy school-child? Come to that, what happens to the people who drive them today? The driver-operated bus that has emerged in recent years already consumes large amounts of time by dealing with the issue of tickets, a task formerly undertaken by a conductor, whilst the bus was on the move.

If computers were introduced everywhere, even when they were entirely superfluous, then we could lose out on a large amount of human contact and human activity. It was recently reported that the Reverend Ronald Jaenisch, of Sunnydale, California had programmed a micro-computer to recite the entire wedding ceremony. Electronic bed-mates must be next.

An example of the feasibility of making a computer-run home is the automatic house built by the Sharp Corporation at Nara, the ancient Japanese capital city. There is a central console in the kitchen which displays which curtains are open, which windows, what lamps are on; the temperature outside is displayed, and the temperature in each of the rooms is easily regulated at the touch of a button. More than seventy percent of the energy for this house comes from solar panels on the roof, and insulation levels are high, so retaining the heat from within (remembering that a single person gives out as much heat as a 100-watt heater).

The radio and television, record player, tape-recorder and video equipment are all controlled by the computer. A series of warning systems gives notice of the entry of a burglar or the outbreak of fire. There is even a television screen which Sharp have perfected which enables you to call up nine different images at once (thus making it possible for the family to watch different programmes on TV at the same time and, what's more, on the same set).

Many time-wasting occupations can usefully be controlled by automatic devices like micro-computers in the future. But two points must be borne in mind:
1. There is no virtue in trying to automate procedures that are themselves enjoyable, or which involve human communication.
2. There is no need for you to feel 'inferior' if you do not know how to program a machine yourself. You do not need a degree in mechanical engineering to know how to drive a car, any more than you need to be expert at printing and bookbinding to enjoy a novel.

Must I be able to type before I can use a computer?

To use a terminal for such tasks as entering answers to multiple-choice questions (like 'PRESS THE BUTTON TO OBTAIN THE SUM INDICATED: £10, £25, £50'), or to order cheque-books from a terminal at the bank, you do not have to do anything other than read and push buttons. If you wish to start

3

programming your machine, however, then the answer clearly is yes. People who want to become hands-on programmers must be able to use the keyboard efficiently. But the conventional QWERTY keyboard, which most people find hard to understand until they get used to it, is not the only kind of input available. One updated version is the Maltron keyboard in which the keys are set in curved rows that fit the position of the fingers. Standard keyboards, being based on rectangular arrays of square buttons, force the hand to conform, but the Maltron does the converse.

There are four or five rows of buttons for each hand (not to be vague, but there are three columns of four rows and three columns of five rows), with two added groups of buttons alongside, five of them for the right hand and four for the left; whilst beneath these irregular configurations there are two groups, each of eight buttons, which lie beneath the thumbs.

Gone is the QWERTY format, which was designed only to stop the type bars from catching against each other in the first slow, manual typewriters. In the Maltron system letters such as *t, h, o,* and *r* lie beneath the strongest fingers of the right hand, and *a, n, i* and *s* lie beneath the fingers of the left. The weight of the hand is supported by resting the ball against an upraised portion of the keyboard frame, and the alignment of the keys themselves is perfectly comfortable.

Naturally a system like this flies in the face of the orthodox version, and it will be a long time before it can be incorporated into everyday teaching schedules at schools and colleges. But the Maltron is worth watching, and stands a good chance of becoming popular in the next decade or two.

A considerably more unusual system is the Microwriter. This is a hand-held device, which is similarly built to accommodate fingers in a relaxed position. About the size of two packets of cigarettes, the Microwriter bears four buttons in line with the finger-tips of the right hand, and two additional buttons which act as keys for the thumb. At the top of the device is a strip of liquid crystal diode components which show the results.

The idea behind the Microwriter is to generate letters by pressing the keys in specific patterns. Not only is it a 'letter form generator', the Microwriter also has an inbuilt memory of about the equivalent of four typed pages of A4, and it can also be connected ('interface') with a computer, so facilitating storage, the possibility of word processing at a later date, or printout through any of the normal means.

If you are coming to computers fresh and untrammelled by the restrictions of conventional typing skills, then this might be just the product. Experienced users say that, although you do have to master the combinations of buttons that correspond to the various characters you wish to type, this is no more tedious than learning to type the ordinary way. Against the Microwriter is the fact that it costs more than the cheapest computers.

The ultimate in systems for communicating with computers would of course be a machine that responded to the spoken word. There are several research teams around the world wrestling with the possibility, but the

4

nearest to the solution so far seem to be Plessey, who are co-operating with research scientists from Imperial College London, and the universities of Loughborough and Edinburgh. Research began in the autumn of 1983, starting with the assumption that the human voice is able to produce 130 separate speech sounds, and from there building a program that can interpret sounds, break them down into their recognisable components, and match those with its own memory, before printing out the result. Regional variations of accent should pose no problem once the machine is in operation, for the team would formulate a standard text which a new user would read, so re-programming that sector of the memory for the new sound of those words.

Naturally, that problem only arises when the first successful experiments have been completed. But the end result would be that you would be able to talk to a computer at around dictation speed, and have the result typed out immediately. Ambiguity, ever-present in any language, may prove the greatest obstacle. Everyone has their own classic tale of misunderstanding. I remember once when a distinguished academic rang and spoke to my secretary. 'Hello,' he said, 'Cairns-Smith here.' The secretary, always friendly even when faced with an unfamiliar name, did not flinch. 'Hello, Ken,' she replied brightly. Or what of the occasion when I visited someone whose name I had noted as Mr Ville? It was Miss de Ville all the while. But just say those two out loud, and see how easy they are to confuse.

However, this is exactly the point, say the proponents of speech-mediated typewriters. There is no point in raising objections to the accuracy of such a device when we make such mistakes ourselves during everyday life. Few typed-out passages from dictation or an audio cassette are entirely free from mistakes, and if we are so fallible then a machine must surely be excused. What would happen then is that the dictation would be translated into a form suitable for a word-processor, and the mistakes would be edited out. Reading through a text and marking up the occasional transcription error is no new task.

How powerful are micro-computers?

The first miniaturised computer to use the integrated circuit — the Intel 4004 — was not a personal computer in the modern sense. It was designed for strictly scientific applications. But it embodied the equivalent power of more than two thousand transistors. Just twenty-three years before it appeared, headlines had been written about the famous ENIAC device, which had weighed thirty tons: and now there was a handy computer with the same computing capacity as that!

It is difficult to convey any real idea of the progress in the field since. Calculating power has increased as costs have fallen, until we have now reached the stage where, if the same progress had been made in the aviation business, you could buy a light aircraft for £2 which would have the performance of the Concorde. . . .

5

What is a program? Is it any different from a mathematical problem?

Yes, it is. A problem is simply a mathematical expression with an answer, whilst a program is a series of steps which help to solve a problem.

Here is an example. Suppose you are using a computer and programming it in the most commonly known 'language', BASIC. You could type in the following:

PRINT 25 + 40

Then press the ENTER key or the RETURN key (depending on the system, the manual will tell you which it is), and the answer will at once appear on the screen in the form:

65

If that seems rather bald, then you could pad it out by instructing the computer to print out the question as well as the answer. In this language, the way you feed in this instruction is to insert quote marks " " around the portion that should be printed out on the screen. The problem would then be:

PRINT   "25 + 40 = " 25 + 40

and what appears on the screen becomes:

25 + 40 = 65

The insertion of those inverted commas means that the computer took what was between them as a 'string', i.e. a series of characters to be simply printed out. The fact that they were also a mathematical problem is irrelevant to the computer, which merely does exactly what you tell it.

The second part of that expression, however, is not included in the inverted commas, but is a simple addition sum: 25 + 40. This the computer recognises as a set of figures looking for an answer, and so it prints the answer for you.

In fact, both of these operations are programs of a sort, but they tackle the problem in much the same way as a calculator, only with the possibility of printing the question as well as the answer. To present this in the form of an authentic-looking program, however, we have to set out the problem in the current sequence and using the appropriate conventions. Again, using BASIC, this is:

```
10 REM Program to show addition of 25 to 40
20 PRINT "25 + 40 = " 25 + 40
30 END
```

Note that the numbering of the stages has been done in tens, not units, since this makes it easier to add steps to a program (see p. 000). The first step is numbered 10, and then follows the statement REM, which is an abbreviation for REMARKS, and is the line in which you make a statement for your own reference. The computer takes no action on these words. (Nor does it have any way of knowing what they 'mean'.) You then type in the title of the program.

The next stage is numbered 20 (not 2, or 11) and you then instruct the computer *firstly* to print out the expression *25 plus 40 equals*, and *secondly* — as a second operation — to solve this problem 25 + 40 =. The third stage (numbered 30) shows that this is the end of the operation.

After you have entered this, all you do is press the key labelled RUN, which tells the computer to run the program. It will print up the problem, add the solution, and you will have had the immense satisfaction of seeing the computer work through a program of your own. At that moment, you stop being a calculator and become a genuine computer programmer. Even if it is still early days, and you could have solved the problem itself in your head in a fraction of the time.

Why 'program'?

It was once 'programme', of course. But there has to be some sense of international accord, and 'program' is the American version of the word. It is worth adopting elsewhere partly because the United States has become the focus of Western electronic research, partly because the use of the term in computerese is a distinct word and can usefully be distinguished from its counterpart, and partly because it is shorter and more economical to write. Language is, in any event, a changing phenomenon, and nobody should object to new terms like this taking hold, although this is not to say that the neologisms of the computer freak should invade everyday English. 'Program' may be a justifiable introduction — a legitimate word with a specific meaning — but there are other usages that are essentially illiterate or ungrammatical. The use of the plural term 'data' as though it were singular is an example of this. Everywhere in science it is 'one datum, several data'; but computer freaks use 'data' in the singular, just as fey marketing men have popularised 'the media' as a singular noun.

Why do noughts have lines across them?

That is because you need to distinguish zero's from capital letter O's. There are added problems in drawing distinctions between the number 1, the initial letter I, and the small letter l. Fortunately, the context in which these three hard-to-distinguish entities occur makes them distinguishable. Meanwhile for computer purposes, there is some sense in adopting 0 and Ø to save confusion. There is just one small complication, and that is that there is a *letter Ø* in many languages. In the Scandinavian literature, for instance 0 would always mean a figure, whilst Ø would be a letter — exactly the converse of the cosily detached conventions of computer people.

What are software and hardware?

The hardware is the equipment you buy, such as the computer itself. The software is the set of instructions you give it — the program. You do not need much in the way of hardware to make your own software, given the right degree of application and producing programs can be a highly profitable business these days.

Even schoolchildren have made a tidy income from the writing of programs, often for video games, and it costs very little to set up as a software originator. But much of the software available for today's computers is unsatisfactory for a number of reasons: it can be too complex, or too limited in scope for the average user. Alternatively it can be inaccurately written — i.e., it contains bugs which the buyer of a package should not expect to find in the finished product — and it is often, as one regular user put it to me, 'downright illiterate'. It is important to see software running before you buy it. Just because it is flashily packaged, it does not follow that it works satisfactorily.

What are ROM and RAM?

This is where the jargon starts. Computer buffs bandy ROM and RAM like the names of old friends. They are, in fact, nothing more baffling than two kinds of computer memory. ROM stands for 'Read-only Memory'. It is a memory store which is made by a manufacturer and contains a mass of data for a computer. The data can be read only, but not altered. RAM means 'Random Access Memory'. This is the memory of a computer which stores whatever you have just typed in on the keyboard. It is a temporary memory, whereas ROM is permanent. Cut off the power in mid-calculation and all the RAM disappears (for this reason it is often called 'volatile' memory, since a power-cut makes it evaporate). So data that are in some fairly final stage of processing, or which are needed for the future, are usually transferred to a separate store — a cassette or a disk (see p. 26).

You would use a RAM facility for recalling addresses, for example, which you had entered in a list. ROM would hold permanent operational details, like a vocabulary or word-processing system.

There is also EPROM, which holds data just like a ROM system, but which can be altered by re-programming. The initials stand for 'Erasable Programmable ROM'.

8

2 Pre-history — The World B.C.*

How old is the principle of rapid data-handling?

Rapid ways of handling figures rely on simplifying the quantities and making them easier to handle. One very ancient version is the abacus. Here, beads on wires or in grooves represent digits. By moving a specific bead from one end of a groove, or wire, to the other, you can bring it into a calculation or eliminate it. Experienced users of these deceptively simple devices can carry out complex calculations at astonishing speed, and they are still widely used. Nothing is stranger than to see a Soviet newspaper-seller in his kiosk working out complex additions with an abacus faster than I could ever match him with the calculator on my wristwatch. Though the principle is an ancient one, it is by much the same principle that a computer handles data. It would not be accurate to say that we should regard the 1's and 0's which are the computer's mainstay in all its calculations as simply beads in different positions, for the similarity is not that close. But the two ideas have much in common, and in one sense the idea of the abacus stemmed from the same mentality as the modern computer concept.

What exactly does 'digital' mean?

A digital device is any kind of device which is concerned with numbers. The word comes originally from the digits with which, as a child, you began to count.

There are basically two ways of looking at a quantity, or measuring a change. One of them is when the phenomenon in which you are interested is changed to an analogy of some kind, which makes it easier to interpret. For instance, it might be the modelling of the passing of an hour by having a hand move round the dial of a watch. It could be the transformation of the temperature in a room to the length of liquid in the stem of a thermometer. A sundial is even such a device, for it converts the movement of the sun into a shadow against a scale.

*B.C. = Before Computers.

9

These systems are all known as *analog* systems. A watch with hour and minute hands is an analog watch, because the movement of the hands is an analogy to the passing of time. The amount of time that has passed is measured in a purely arbitrary way, of course. There is no such thing in Nature as an hour.

The alternative way of displaying the same data is to record a changing digit as time goes by. This is exactly what a digital watch does. Universally popular, ridiculously cheap to manufacture, digital watches make their counterpart, the analog watch, seem traditional and rather old-fashioned by comparison.

In fact, for all their admitted novelty and their relative accuracy, digital watches have not succeeded in replacing analog watches altogether. One of the great reasons is that any analog timepiece gives a much better indication of the passing of time. Trying to time a broadcast, for example, and to keep an eye on the passing of ten seconds, is extraordinarily difficult if you have your eye on a digital clock, because the changing numbers do not signify anything conceptual. An analog clock, by comparison, shows the hand moving progressively around the dial and demonstrates the passage of time so clearly that it is very much easier to know where you are.

Analog data are often converted into digital form, so that they are amenable to computer analysis. And these days it is not uncommon to see digital data printed out in analog form. The eye is often unable to perceive the pattern in a table of data, for example, but printed out on a graphic display as a graph or a histogram, relationships can easily emerge.

Who invented the calculator?

The abacus, dating back several thousand years, was clearly the first simplified means of calculating without figures. But in the history of calculation, there is one undoubtedly important name, that of Blaise Pascal because he built the first desk-top mechanical calculator in 1642.

Pascal was a French mathematician and philosopher, who set out to make a mechanical means of adding currency. At the time, the franc did not exist; the units were the *livre*, divided into twenty units known as the sol, each of which was divided into twelve deniers. (This is a parallel to the old English system of pounds, shillings and pence, and the French used the initials £ s d for their own currency at that time, too.)

His calculator was 36 centimetres long, shaped like a pencil-box. It contained a row of cogs, each of which was linked to its neighbour by a mechanism which was geared to the ratio between one digit and the next (e.g. twelve to one when moving from sol to denier). There was an extra ratchet to enable the calculator to carry a number from one column to the next. By turning the wheels on the front of the device with a stylus, to give the figures it was desired to add, the corresponding total emerged through a row of rectangular windows, one above each wheel. In this way you could dial in a figure, add another to it mechanically, and note down the result. Subtraction was more difficult, but the machine was intended for addition and in that application it was a success.

However, an adding machine as such cannot really be called a proper calculator. It fell to a German named Gottfried Wilhelm von Leibnitz to perfect the idea. He knew that the principal difficulty with Pascal's machine was that the only way to perform multiplication was to add a given number to itself several times, each time re-entering the same figure. It was a tiresome business.

Leibnitz replaced the concept of gear-wheels with stepped gears cut into a roller. There were nine rows of gear teeth, representing the numbers 1 to 9. Each successive tooth was longer than the last, and so a neighbouring gear could be slid along the length of the roller, as well as merely engaging with all nine. This made it possible to introduce multiplication into the system. With Leibnitz's original calculator, it was only necessary to enter a given number once, and then to turn the handle a given number of times to display the answer. Until the electronic calculator began to enter circulation, this form of desk-top machine was very common. The machines used in shops right up to the early 1970s had much in common with Leibnitz's design dating back two and three-quarter centuries before.

Where did the word computer originate?

It arose in the mid-seventeenth century, and was then used to describe a person who calculated. Surveyors and astronomers had a 'computer' to work out their sums. The word began to emerge in the electronics field in 1937 when a Cambridge mathematician, Alan Turing, wrote a paper on 'Computable Numbers' which described a universal 'automaton' which could be used for the solution of logical problems. During the years of the Second World War, the word was first applied to the forerunners of today's devices, such as EDVAC — justly abbreviated from the mouthful it stood for, the Electronic Discrete Variable Automatic Computer — of 1945. Since then the term has steadily grown in familiarity. Is it possible that anybody in the Western world has not heard of computers yet?

Which was the first computer?

History agrees that the first-ever recognisable computer was the 'difference engine', invented by an eccentric and highly-strung mathematician, Charles Babbage, in the 1820s. The difference engine was a complex system of carefully machined wheels and levers. From this, Babbage planned to build a much more ambitious 'analytical engine', which would have been the size of a playing-field, powered by several vast steam-engines, and requiring a huge array of belts, pulleys, wheels and gears to function correctly. It was ahead of its time, needing the precision of modern technology, not the massive and disaster-prone products of Victorian engineering, to make it work properly.

Babbage himself was an obsessive man, and relied on his friendship with Lord Byron's daughter Ada, Countess of Lovelace. She provided him with encouragement and much financial support, and became his advocate in the public arena. No one understood the potential of his machine better than she did, and Lady Lovelace was a perfect public relations representative for Babbage. At one time, to raise money for the analytical engine, they decided to use Babbage's existing machine as a means of predicting the outcome of horse races. Between them, he and Lady Lovelace lost thousands of pounds. In the end, the analytical engine remains nothing more than a vast collection of diagrams and working drawings.

Babbage was also the inventor of the cow-catcher for steam trains, was father of the speedometer, and of the first reliable tables of life expectancy; but he worked for forty years on plans for his great analytical engine, which had all the hallmarks of a modern-day computer. Babbage died in 1871, famous in his later years for an unceasing campaign against the loud music that assaulted him and penetrated through the walls. (Was he even here anticipating today's disaffected neighbours who complain about hi-fi racks playing full blast — although in his day, the source of his annoyance was the barrel organ?)

The first successful computer-like device to be produced was made in Sweden in 1843, by Per Georg Scheutz and his son Eduard. It was a version of the Babbage 'difference engine'. But whereas Babbage was never able to make a full-size version of his device, the Scheutzes used rather different mechanical systems, and they did succeed. Machines derived from their ideas were produced for scores of years subsequently, and were used throughout the Victorian era.

Where do punched cards fit in?

There are two varieties of this idea you may have encountered. The first is a means of sorting cards in a file index, but with the possibility of drawing out items which conform to specific demands. The second is a kind of thin post-card perforated with small rectangular windows, by which data can be entered into a computer and the results stored.

Perforated filing cards are very useful. Each card has a corner cut off, so that the cards can be stacked up oriented in the same way. On each card you enter the details you wish to retrieve at a future date. It might be, say, books you have read. You would give the full details, author, title, date of publication, publisher, place etc; perhaps also the source of the book — its library details, shelf number or whatever.

You would then list a series of options by which you might wish to locate

12

those details in the future: was the book for children, a thriller, illustrated, fiction, reference, good or bad . . . whatever you wished to select. Around the card edge there is a series of punched holes, and the card is pre-printed with a number against each one. What you do is to associate each numbered hole with a selection characteristic. Thus hole No. 1 might represent a book for children, No. 2 a book for teenagers, No. 3 for young adults . . . and so on.

What you then do is to cut away the card between the hole and the edge, at each numbered perforation which corresponds to the book in question. Thus, if this is the way your index has been drawn up, you might cut away holes numbered 2, 13, 24 and 25 if the book was for teenagers, well illustrated, historical, and well written.

Picking out the card or cards that corresponds to those demands is now a simple matter. A knitting needle is inserted through all the holes numbered 2, 13, 24 and 25. Once the four needles are in place, you pick up the whole lot — cards, needles and all — and shake. All the cards where the holes have been cut away at the indicated positions will now drop from the file into the tray beneath. A quick shake to make sure none remain, and you now have in front of you all the books in your index which correspond to those factors. You then select the books from that short-list and eventually all the cards are put back into the stack, with the cut-away corner in the matching position so that the holes are all lined up for the next time they are used.

This is a simple sorting system which many people might still find of value. A lot of computer work involves exactly this kind of selection, and the use of an expensive machine with its time-consuming methods of adding and selecting entries could well be obviated by this cheap and manual alternative. There are few means of filing books, reprints, letters, postcards, photographic negatives, personal likes and dislikes amongst the customers of a business, menu cards etc. which are so simple, so cheap, and so foolproof. A power cut causes them no problem, either.

The second kind of punched card does not merely have perforations around the edge, but windows across the centre. This is the kind of card that was often supplied with credit-account statements, but the system is going out of use these days as it is slow for many applications. The idea of a punched card to hold complicated data is not in itself a new one. The piano roll of an automatic piano-player is an example of the way in which this kind of perforation system can be used to store data over a long period of time. Today, for instance, it is possible to lace up a piano-player with a roll cut scores of years before by a now-dead musician and recreate the notes in exactly the order in which the composer wanted them. Tone, touch and finesse are not part of the system, it is true; but none the less the recreation of music from a long punched-card system is a familiar model of the system with which we are concerned.

The idea began in Lyon, France with the invention of Joseph-Marie Jacquard around 1800. He was a silk weaver, the son of a family traditionally involved in that craft, and he set out to automate the pattern-making process in ornamental cloth. Jacquard knew that the difficult part of the process was lifting specific threads in the loom as the shuttle passed through, in order to build up — line by line — the complexity of the finished pattern.

Jacquard's breakthrough was the first punched card system. He cut the pattern in the form of slots in a card, each slot corresponding to the position of a lever which could be lifted when desired at each pass of the shuttle. Once the card had been cut correctly, it became the permanent embodiment of a stage in the weaving process, and as the cards passed through the automatic loom (just like the fan-folded piano roll) the weaving of the pattern was controlled without any possibility of an error of judgment, a lapse of memory or of concentration. The result was a reliable and inexpensive form of weaving of unprecedentedly high quality.

Jacquard first exhibited this remarkable development in 1801. He tried to introduce it into general use in Lyon, but was mobbed by workers who were aware that such a development could threaten their livelihood. In one attack Jacquard almost lost his life. Eventually the importance to industry of this development was recognised and the French government awarded him a pension, with which he lived for the rest of his life in comfort and dignity. He died in 1834 at the age of eighty-two.

Clearly the social implications of Jacquard's development were far-reaching, though it is fair to say that his work was responsible for the mushrooming development in the status of Lyon, now France's most civilised city in the minds of many people. (Well, I adore it anyhow.) And exploring the tunnel-like *traboules* (the passageways through the old houses in the weaving quarter) and the old weaving shops where punched cards were first used is a delight.

Jacquard was the first person commercially to apply the punched card system (the idea had first been proposed by Bouchon and Falcon some years before) but his system clearly had widespread potential and it was recognised as such by Babbage, in his own experimental work. However it fell to Herman Hollerith, a US citizen of German background, to exploit the principle on the grand scale. He worked for the Bureau of the Census, and had the idea to use punched cards as a means of collating data for the government.

Hollerith realised that punched cards made it easy to enter data of a wide range of different types by punching holes in cards, and went on to show how they could then be classified, sorted and stored for a variety of purposes. His system was first used for the US census of 1890. Subsequently he founded a company to make automated accountancy equipment, and that company went on to become the International Business Corporation, known better today, perhaps, as IBM.

The punched card which became so familiar was based on Hollerith's original ideas, and the usual version of the card was capable of holding 80 characters, each represented by combinations of holes punched in the card. The code (by which you could read back a punched card in your possession) was as follows:

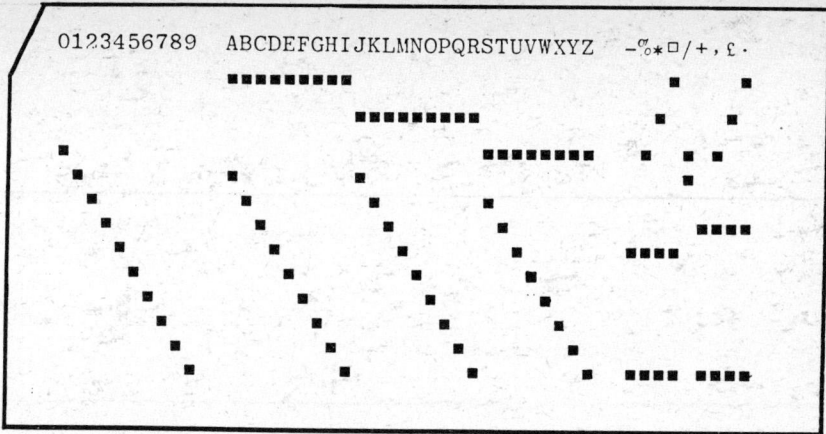

The punched card code

Nowadays the punched card system is being replaced by faster methods of handling data and storing information. Not only is the system slow, but it has an inherent inflexibility. Each card requires twelve rows of eighty characters, and though that might work well in certain circumstances it is useless in others. It is well-matched to the needs of the US census office, for example, for the number of data you might wish to record will be much the same in the case of one person as with the next. But in other applications you might need to record a large amount of data in one case (which would be too much to store on a single card), and just a couple of figures in another (for which you would still have to waste a whole card).

One interesting consequence of the eighty-character line used by the IBM punched card system is that many modern micro-computers have screens and other facilities which work on the eighty-character system. So, though the card seems to be almost extinct now, its legacy lives on. There are plenty of modern computer users who complain about the inflexibility which faces them in consequence.

When did the first micro-computer appear?

The micro-computer was made possible by the appearance of the integrated circuit which was invented in 1959. I wrote a youthful article about it at the time, in which I said that it meant 'transistors were obsolete', but the whole implication of that seemed unimaginable at the time. It meant that the tiny transistor radio was going to be replaced by something much tinier again, for one thing (that was what appealed most to the young mind at the time) and that computers could get smaller, too. I used to use something called an Elliott 803 in the mid-1960s, a computer which filled a room with humming electronics and clacking printers, and we all knew that one day it would become considerably smaller . . . but nobody realised how far it would go.

The growing interest in miniaturised electronic systems meant that the first do-it-yourself desk-top computer appeared on the front cover of a hobby magazine in Autumn 1974 (a scant decade before the time when I am writing these words!). It was a home-assemble computer named the ALTAIR 8800, and bore little resemblance to the sleek desk-top micro of today. It had a series of switches for the input of data, for there was no monitor screen or keyboard in this pioneering model.

Which was the first great computer?

This was ENIAC. The initials stood for Electronic Numerical Integrator and Calculator and it was completed in 1946, at the University of Pennsylvania. It occupied more than 2,000 square feet of floor area and contained some 18,000 electronic valves. It could undertake 5,000 addition calculations per second, powered by a pulse generator at the heart of the machine which produced a steady 100,000 pulses per second. The shape (in other words, the wave-form) of each pulse could be modified to correspond to the encoded data, and so ENIAC was 1000 times faster in operation than any of its contemporaries.

ENIAC did not use the binary codes which are at the heart of all modern computer operation (see p. 000 for an explanation of their working). Life would have been much simpler for the technicians if it had. Instead, each digit was fed into a ring circuit linking ten valves, one each corresponding to figures from zero to nine. Only one of the valves was in the 'on' mode at a time, corresponding to the figure it was meant to represent. Each time a pulse was received by the circuit, that lamp turned 'off' and the next one was activated in its place. When it was time to transmit data, rather than store it, a series of pulses would be generated corresponding to each level above zero that the lamps in the ring circuits had reached.

It had taken ten engineers two and a half years to build ENIAC, yet to change the programming was a complicated procedure. Sections of the input had to be physically rewired each time the program was to be altered. And of course the appearance of the transistor just two years after ENIAC came into operation marked the demise of the gigantic valve computer. However, ENIAC deserves to be remembered for its place as the first mainframe computer in history.

Also worth a place in our memories is EDSAC, which was built at the University of Cambridge between the years 1946 and 1949. This was the first computer to have a stored program. In that sense it was a true predecessor to the desk-top micro of today. And its timing was perfectly matched to the emergence of solid-state physics as a major feature of development.

16

3 Home Truths – Buying and Installing Your Own Micro

How do I choose a micro?

The single most important point to remember is that you should avoid being bowled over, by salesmanship, by advertising, even by persuasion. There are certain pressures behind the way computers are sold which you need to know about before you start.

To begin with, there is an understandable inclination towards more expensive equipment, when the seller is asked for advice. Sellers live on their mark-up, so there is no great advantage to the retail outlet of endlessly recommending cheap apparatus. The pioneering Sinclair ZX81 was the computer which started off the home enthusiast back in 1981. After a few years it began to seem relatively old-fashioned, but it was then priced at a mere £45, a price to include a memory expansion pack. It was an astonishing bargain, but few retailers were going to press open-eyed tyro purchasers into being satisfied with that when there were more costly items to sell.

On the other hand, there are examples of computers which are available in two versions, and there is the clear temptation to purchase the costlier of the two before you are sure whether its added advantages are really worth-while. The main advantage of the BBC micro, by Acorn, is that it can be up-graded for use as a full business micro. That – at a selling price of £400 – is a fair price. Many of them have been sold to households where there is a partial business use in view.

But Acorn also produced a smaller version, the Electron computer, selling at less than half the price. It had the same size memory (32K) as the BBC version, but had cut out many of the extras. Gone were the plugs and sockets for connection to peripherals, for instance. Gone too was the ON/OFF switch, making it necessary for the user to turn the computer off at the wall socket. But for most users, the Acorn model was all that was required. However, how many salesmen impressed this on prospective purchasers?

The important facts to bear in mind when you decide to purchase a micro of your own are:

1. What jobs do I want it to perform?

Why not write out a list of applications (accounts, horse-racing predictions, mortgage calculations, colour graphics, etc.) and take that along when you go to buy? You can then be certain that the software exists before you decide on a model which may turn out to have some vital component missing.

2. How much should I spend?

The best way here is to talk to enthusiasts and to read the current computer magazines. Also check through the discount warehouse catalogues and advertisements, to see who has what on offer.

3. Is the machine obsolescent?

Do check that the device is not a model that is now out of date. New devices appear so often that it is worth keeping up with computer news *before* you enter the shop; on the other hand (as in the case of the Sinclair ZX81) there are cases of a perfectly usable computer being sold off to clear stocks.

4. What peripherals are there?

'Peripherals' are what in another world you would call gadgets or accessories. They are the things that connect to the computer in order to expand its usability: printers, memories, keyboards, a joy-stick for graphics and games.

5. What else do I have to buy?

Check carefully here. You do not want to get home only to find that you still need to purchase other equipment before you can use the machine properly. If you need a cassette to input a particular program, do not wait until after you have returned home to discover the fact. Make sure that you have the correct plugs for the sockets you want to use. See that there is a full manual, and a setting-up program. If you want to use the computer as a word processor, then ensure that you have the relevant word-processing software before you settle on the purchase. Nothing would be more frustrating than getting home and being unable to do what you had set your heart on.

Much worse is the sad fact that, if a computer does not measure up to your demands, then you may well have to buy more of the unwanted manufacturer's products to try and save the day. This can be an ascending spiral of cost and disillusionment. The answer is *always* to watch a demonstration of *exactly* what you want to do on the machine of your choice, but in the store. One factor in the purchaser's favour is the mounting competition for his cash, as retailers and models of micros proliferate. Some shops and manufacturers are being nudged into a more enlightened view, and at least one manufacturer now offers a trial on a 'take it home for 48 hours' basis. This is potentially the best solution of all, *if* you have the experience, or the experience of a friend who can help you, to take advantage of it.

6. And don't forget:
The answers to questions like these could make all the difference between
coming to know the joy of computers, and a world of pain and frustration. Is
there a nearby computer club? Where is the branch of the users' club for the
model you have in mind? Are there any training programmes available?
What about evening classes? What service and after-sales arrangements are
in existence where you live? How long do engineers take to come out on a
call? What advice would experienced users offer you? Is there a local store
that provides reliable advice? Are the manufacturers of your own chosen
machine reliable? Is the company secure, or might it go bankrupt just when
you need further equipment? How long are waiting lists for delivery of what
you have in mind? Is your machine a sturdy one? How fast does it operate?
What are its graphics capabilities? How controllable is the rate of scroll? How
easy is it to expand it? Can it be upgraded? Will your family mind? Can you
afford to be without a computer? Can you pay the price of owning one?

Can a micro-computer work with any TV?

No. Some are rather particular. Always check the compatibility of your set
before you buy your hardware; if the computer fails to work on your colour
TV at home, then take the computer into a nearby store and ask to see it
connected up to other makes of television set. That may well reveal an
incompatibility. Then you can have hours of fun deciding whether to change
the computer, or buy a new TV. A new range of high-resolution televisions is
expected to be launched in the 1990's, which will make today's picture look
grainy by comparison. Cable, incidentally, may make less of an impact than
many imagine. One estimate says that in 1990 there may be fewer cable
outlets at home than there were in 1980. So keep an eye on the future
before you invest.

If I buy a micro-computer, how do I set it up?

Everyone should regard the dining-room table as their first computer bench.
This is a long-standing tradition, at least two or three years old (which is as
long a time in computer terms as a week is in politics). So unpack the device
on the dining-room table, opening the box carefully. You can store it in the
loft. In fact you can store it anywhere, but do store it, because you will need it
if you are going to return the equipment to the shop or send it away for any
reason. Keep all the specially-shaped packing materials, like moulded
polystyrene blocks, for the same reason.
   The first task is to read the check-list in the user's manual and carefully
identify all the components in the box(es) you have brought home. Make
sure it is all there before you begin. If anything is wrong, then go back to the

19

shop (with the purchase documents) straight away. If that is not possible, then take a photograph of the equipment as unpacked, to illustrate the nature of your complaint.

Read through the manual, in order to become acquainted with the bits and pieces before you. Then read it again. It is important to feel that you know what everything *is*, and where it is all supposed to go. In particular, inspect the computer itself from all aspects, identifying which controls and which sockets perform which functions. Before the device is connected up, you should at least feel that you know your way round it easily enough.

If a cable does not connect to its socket, then check that you have the right one, and not something which looks similar to the eye. Ensure that the pins are correctly aligned (some sockets are meant to connect correctly only when offered up in exactly the right positions). Do not force components into slots; they may be going in backwards. Check again with the manual if you are at all unsure, or ring the shop if in further doubt. Of course, you may have had a full demonstration by the retailer and if such is the case then mistakes or uncertainties should not arise as frequently as if you are a complete newcomer to the machine itself.

Connect the plug to the power cable last of all, and switch on at the mains. Then (unless your computer does not have an on/off switch) switch on the instrument itself. When you switch on, there is often an audible 'bleep' and a signal light will come on. Other lights will come on too, if you have peripherals plugged in. On the screen may well appear the manufacturer's trade name or a welcoming message. The computer itself may hum gently in a reassuringly space-age fashion.

If the screen remains blank, remember to try turning up the brightness. That may be the immediate answer. Alternatively, check that all the connections are secure. See that the mains has been switched on, that the plug is home firmly; and in the last resort that there has not been a blown fuse — or even a power cut.

Once the computer is in action, open the disk drive or the cassette player, insert the manufacturer's program, and from then on it will indicate what you should do. If it is taken methodically, as computer matters always must be, then the installation and setting up of your own micro should prove to be entirely painless. Once hooked — away you go.

Can a computer fit into my living room?

It certainly can. Much thought has gone into making home computers look attractive, and they compare well enough with colour television sets, rack systems, speaker units and video-recorders. There is a trend today to re-designate a living room filled with this kind of technology as a 'media-room'. It is an appropriate, if trendy, name. However, the abandonment of the word 'living' can easily hint to an abandonment of much of the *activity* of 'living', too. Always remember that the term 'media', even when it is used, as it often is nowadays, as the singular noun it manifestly is not, began life as the 'mass media of communication'. The fact that we have lost the 'communication' from that phrase at about the same time as we began to lose out on *actual* 'communication' between ourselves is another pointed coincidence.

A computer can be used as a focus of entertainment and information, it can generate games for long evenings, summon up factual data for visitors anxious to book a late holiday or check a recipe. It is important to make sure it is installed away from competing electrical equipment, away from radiators and windows, and in a safe place where it will not be knocked over, nor sprinkled with coffee or cigarette ash. The possibility of protecting it with a dust-cover is worth bearing in mind, and there are many purpose-built desk or table units which house a computer and a few basic peripherals in a single item of furniture of pleasing design.

So the computer can actually become part of the daily furniture of the room, used as a routine item of equipment like a washing-machine, a lawn-mower or a reel-to-reel tape-recorder used by a Tamla Motown freak.

Should I simply buy a micro that plugs into the television?

In terms of cost, if a low level of use is all you require, the answer is yes. But if you think about it you will see that this answer is deceptively simple.

Television sets are designed to be looked at from across the room, with the viewer on the sofa and the TV on its table at the other side of the hearthrug. The micro's VDU — the visual display unit — by contrast, is looked at from a far shorter distance. The front surface of a television tube is traditionally made of polished glass with a highly reflective surface and in the siting of TV sets in the home this is rarely obtrusive. VDU screens are made matt, to cut down reflections, since in the way they are used, reflections matter far more.

Finally, because of the distance between the viewer and the TV set, a television has no need to be highly accurate in its depiction of the visual image. The resolution does not need to be notably high. The earlier VHF television sets of the black-and-white era had 405 lines between the top of the screen and the bottom, whilst today's sets have 525 or 625 (depending on whether you live in the USA or the UK). By the time the picture has been composed of the little triads of coloured dots, it is entirely suitable for looking at from across the room, but not so good for a viewer at normal VDU distance. High-resolution monitor screens can produce a picture far finer than we are used to seeing on TV screens.

So there are many reasons why a built-in monitor has advantages over the use of the household TV set as your VDU. On the other hand, the memory demands exerted by a full-colour VDU are considerable. A memory capacity of at least 48K (see p. 56 for an explanation of 'K') is necessary, and 128K RAM is needed for the best resolution on the home computer, such as the British Lynx.

Using the television set is not quite the cut-and-dried solution it appears to be, therefore. Among the other factors to take into consideration, there is also the reaction of the rest of your family to the loss of use of the ordinary TV facility whilst a parent spends long hours programming a system to stock-control the freezer, or a son or daughter tries to make his or her fortune with a new video game in which teachers are caned by the pupils. Peace of mind is an important part of any equation where micros are concerned.

Where should the micro go?

It began on the dining-room table. But if you decide to instal one in your home, it would be as well to decide where it is going to live permanently first. It may be that you intend to use it from time to time, in which case it may well live under its case in the corner of the living-room, like a sewing-machine.

But suppose you opt to instal it in a bedroom or boxroom. What points should be borne in mind? In the first instance, the chosen room should not be damp, nor should it be too dry. It should be warm and cosy. There are reasons for this. Damp conditions cause condensation, whilst a hot, dry, over-centrally-heated atmosphere can generate static, which causes fresh problems.

The room should not contain too many eye-catching objects, nor should it be filled with reflecting surfaces like polished lampshades or pictures on the wall.

The wallpaper should be muted, a strong pattern being distracting to the eye. There should be no brilliant hanging lamp; a muted, diffused light is best, and if it comes from a suspended fitting near the centre of the room an enclosing shade should be chosen to cut down glare.

Angle-poise lamps are a good choice, and so are movable lamp units on track-lighting systems, for they can be angled at will, and changed if the conditions demand it. One popular answer to the problem of lighting a room with a computer is to direct the light upwards, so that it shines onto the ceiling. A sodium vapour lamp has even been suggested, for it is bright, produces a gentle even illumination by the time it has been reflected back from the ceiling, and is a colour that matches well the demands of using a VDU. These lamps can prove complex to instal, however. In principle, try to have bulbs so positioned that your eye does not normally see the light-source direct.

Next, what furniture should go into the room? One intelligent acquisition might be an anti-static sheet to act as a mat for your micro, or to go beneath your chair. Remember that carpets made from man-made fibres generate a lot of static, especially if you walk across them in man-made footwear. So natural espadrilles, apart from being fashionable, make sense, and so does a woollen carpet. Either of these may overcome a static problem, no matter how dry and centrally-heated the room itself might be.

What kind of chair you sit on is obviously important. There is little point in simply sitting in one in a shop, and then assuming it will work well enough at home. Try to sit in it in various positions before you buy it; slump around a little, feel fidgety, move it back and forth, sit there trying to concentrate hard on something nearby which represents the screen. The angle, rake and height are all important, and you may be able to obtain a chair in which all three are adjustable. Castors are often helpful, and so is a swivel. But these features can also be distracting, so make sure you want them before you choose.

Next, the table. There is a code of recommended practice for the use of desk-top computers in Germany (as in other parts of continental Europe) which says that the table height should be 72 cms, but most desks in Britain are a little higher than this, nearer 76 cms. Ideally, the table and the chair should match visually, partly because this creates a more restful atmosphere for the user, but additionally for the appearance of the whole room. It will not be used solely as a computer work-station, after all (remember, ordinary mortals have desks; computer owners and programmers have *work-stations*).

An L-shaped table can be helpful if the computer is to stand alongside a work area or a desk used for organising papers, files or disks. It is possible to buy a purpose-designed bench which has a separate stand for the micro,

The wrong way to set up a micro

The right way to set up a micro

fitted with a swivel and sometimes a tilt control so that the screen can be angled to suit the user and yet can be changed if the position becomes trying.

It *is* important to get hold of a suitable table or desk, since much depends on the degree of comfort and relaxation you can obtain. Remember that the typical keyboard unit can add a further three to five centimetres to the effective height at which you are working, and if the resulting 80 cms is too high for comfort, then a slightly lower table-top — like the German proposal for a height of 72 cms — may be more realistic. Do not be tempted to cut a couple of inches off the bottom of the table legs, though, unless you have to. It would be easier to position a paving slab beneath your chair, or to install a firm cushion above it and a footrest, so that you could adjust the distances until you get used to an ideal position.

The computer itself should be carefully positioned. The biggest problem is the siting of the window. Your computer should not be installed so that you have your back to the window, or you will drown out the VDU with the glare. Do not turn it round, so that you face the window instead, for that is just as bad. In this position your pupils will contract in bright daylight, making the screen itself more difficult to read. The ideal position for the window is to one side. A roller-blind can control the light.

Do not stand the micro itself near a window, either. Sudden changes of

24

temperature can cause problems, rainfall blown in if a window is left open can be damaging to the circuitry. Furthermore, there is no point in advertising the presence of your pride and joy, unless you want to risk it becoming somebody else's.

Computers and radiators are another pair of bad mixers. The temperature of your chosen room should certainly be relatively stable, but the rising heat of a radiator is best avoided.

Once you have installed the machine in its ideal location you must look out for the socket into which the computer will be plugged. You will need several power points at the work-station, inevitably. One to power a typewriter, another for a lamp, and so on. This does *not* mean that everything can go into the same socket through an adaptor, or even alongside it in a triple-gang unit. The surges of current caused as a device is switched on (particularly if it is a high-demand device, like a hairdryer or an iron) can easily upset the computer's running, and a plug-in voltage stabiliser is well worth installing. The best solution is to ensure that the plug for the computer is away from the other plugs you need at the work-station, to avoid voltage competition. Try to keep devices fitted with thermostats out of the way, along with other equipment that generates signal pulses, in case these interrupt the functioning of a program.

When you sit down, there should be a gap of about 20 cms between the bottom of the table and the top of the seat, which leaves your legs room to move. The *top* of the screen should be roughly level with your *chin*, so that you look downwards into the screen at a gentle angle, and your arms should comfortably reach the keyboard.

If any of these factors do not apply, then take a little time to adjust the furniture and the positioning of the computer until you get it right. Comfort is important. Then, when the installation is complete, make sure you 'lose' the trailing cables. Hide them behind racks in shelving, tape them invisibly to the legs of tables, or run them through purpose-built sheaths or cable bridges. Take care running a cable beneath a carpet, for it can easily produce a ridge which will damage the carpet permanently. If you decide to clip a cable to the skirting-board, then run a strip of masking tape along afterwards to improve the appearance and to keep out the dust. Trailing wires and connecting leads are distracting and look unprofessional; they can also be highly dangerous to man and machine.

Finally, what about the comfort of your eyes? Eyestrain is subjective, and is caused by excessive tension of a postural nature as much as by any actual difficulty in seeing. Keep a relaxed posture, and work in bursts with occasional five-minute breaks.

After two or three hours, studying the screen may become more difficult and it is tempting to imagine that your eyes are suffering. The eyes, as such, are not; what is really suffering is the person out of whose head they are peering.

Remember that until middle age, many people can focus easily enough on papers fairly close to and a screen that is 60-odd cms (two feet) away. If you normally wear glasses, then you should wear them for computer work as much as for anything else. Past fifty, though, the eye muscles may find it harder to accommodate changes in focus. Though you may find it easy enough to study the screen, difficulties can arise when you try to look at papers which are lying considerably closer. It is the near-focus which fails.

Given the full story, it is likely that an optician can provide suitable lenses that enable you to continue to work at your computer, hobby or not, without undue strain for as long as you can see anything else clearly. Plenty of people of advanced age (by which I mean in excess of ninety) can see as clearly as they did on the day they first went to school or so they claim, and for them the computer remains crystal-clear.

One final point. People often ask if they can actually damage the eyesight by using a VDU or by straining to see indistinct details. There is not one whit of evidence that looking at things in the wrong way could ever damage the eye itself. If the lens is mismatched to the demands of an occupation, then you may find it hard to concentrate without wearing suitable glasses. But if you *don't* wear the right glasses, or if you *do* keep on staring into that screen, then you cannot — as far as I can tell — ever damage your eyes to the slightest degree.

It is foolish to make yourself tense by failing to take the readily-available precautions that can help us see better — by obtaining ophthalmic advice, for example — but making yourself tense is all you will do. Eye damage is out of the question.

How should I store programs?

In a word, carefully. They cost a lot to purchase. The most long-lasting form in which you might buy a program would be an inflexible disk, whether it took the form of a laser-imprinted digital disk (p. 101) or a hard-disk built into a computer peripheral (p. 68). Next in line would come the cartridges and cassettes. These can be distorted or cracked only if jumped on, and in ordinary use the greatest difficulty might be posed by an accumulation of dust over the years. Cleanliness — hygienic storage — is the answer to that.

Floppy disks — the increasingly popular form of storage for the micro enthusiast — are very much more vulnerable. Good advice is to take your chosen system of storage (a file or a mailing pack) when you go to the shop for a new floppy disk, and put it straight inside. Alternatively, buy both together. The shop assistant will regard you all the better for it: the professional takes greatest care with software.

Damage is one thing, corruption is another. Whereas damage covers mechanical deterioration, breakage, wear or scratching, corruption refers to the degradation of the stored information in the disk or tape itself. There are some apocryphal tales of people who left a disk representing weeks of work at the end of an evening's toil, only to find it had all vanished (the toil, that is, not the disk) next morning.

What does sometimes happen is that a magnetic field produces a change in the recording medium, and irreversibly alters the data stored within it. The principal cause of damage is a field produced by a magnet, followed closely by threats from large electrical coils. The most likely candidate at home would be the field magnet in a loud-speaker system. If you slide a recorded tape across a magnet of that kind, and then remove it, the signal will be partly attenuated, and may even vanish altogether.

The presence of magnetic fields should always be borne in mind when magnetic media are put into store. Keep disk files well away from your hi-fi unit, and never stack cassettes on top of speaker cabinets.

Disks can also be corrupted if they are subjected to electrical interference during operations. If you switch the computer itself off when the disk is in mid-run, you certainly run the risk of corrupting the stored data. And you can produce the same effect — and run the risk of damaging the read/write head of your disk drive unit — by trying to remove the disk whilst it is playing. If it is necessary to stop a disk halfway through, remember always to activate the 'reset' on the system. You may lose some of the data you are processing by so doing, but the disk itself will remain free from corruption.

Never touch the surface of a recording medium. Doing so leaves behind minute traces of moisture and sebaceous oils from the skin. This will not corrupt the disk's stored data, but it can prevent the head from reading the material successfully. If a disk or tape has been compromised in this way, try using a little solvent on a perfectly clean cloth to remove the contamination, first testing for compatibility by treating part of an unwanted tape or disk — the last one you contaminated in this way, perhaps. . . . If the data can then be read correctly, copy the program onto a fresh disk or cassette.

Copying is always a useful safeguard (p. 31). It is sensible practice to run off a copy of any new software as a back-up in case something goes wrong with the original. Disks can be copied onto cassettes, if they are a more realistically-priced option, since although it takes more time you still end up with an 'insurance' copy whilst having the high-speed original available for use.

Data in the RAM are particularly labile, of course. For this reason it makes sense to record information from the RAM at frequent intervals. This is known as 'saving' or 'dumping' the data. Time and experience will show how often you should save data in your own work patterns, but on a word processor, for example, it is usual to save data at the end of each of the pages in the program. At the same time, remember to copy a program on which you have been writing, i.e. to which you have made additions or changes.

Some software is specially programmed to prevent copying in this way. Here you have two options. One is to ask the supplier for a back-up at the time, which they may well offer. The other alternative is a practical one. You simply spend as much time as it takes to work out how to cheat the procedure. For many hackers,* that in itself would amount to a challenge that would keep them out of trouble for many a long evening.

Files can be kept in order like any other storage system, namely by having some identifying 'tag' which specifies it. When you open a new file in your micro, you will find that you are expected to give a name or a number to the topic concerned. There are endless possibilities here. A friend who maintained a disk full of family details, mementos and birthdays called it 'DRAGGOES'. The name given by a landlord who owned student accommodation and kept the details of rents and renewals in this form code-named it 'THE/PITS'. One domestic-accounts file was dubbed 'DOSHDOSH'. Codes can be made as personal and as abtruse as you wish. In some ways it aids security if the word you choose is understandable only by those who need to know it (a family in-joke, for instance).

However, that notion of security is of no value if you keep interesting data on disks which are freely accessible to prying hands, no matter how cleverly tagged each one may be. It is much easier to make off with a revealing floppy disk than it is to take a heavy leather-bound cash-book. So if you have data that has to be kept safely, good computer security is a locked door.

The floppy disks can be kept in a number of ways. The cheapest is to stack them in a box-file, or a plastic holder with a flip-top lid made specially for the

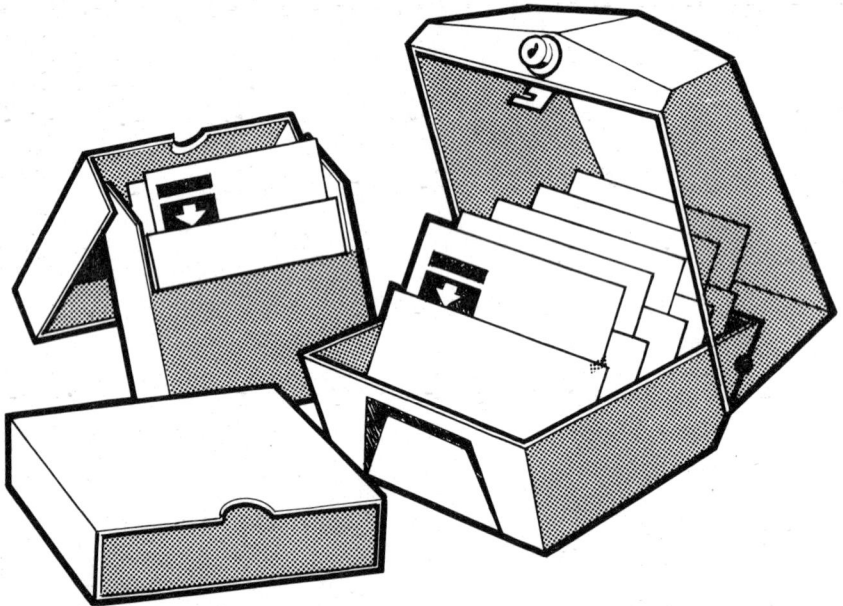

Floppy disk storage

*What one enthusiast calls another.

purpose. Storage in this system is much the same as the way you would keep a collection of singles. For small numbers of disks, when economy is at a premium, this is the easiest answer to the problem.

Next up in terms of complexity and cost is a swinging file system, in which the disks are kept in a series of purpose-built envelopes which locate into a vertically hinged holder. The idea is like those hinged display boards for posters which you find in shops. The advantage here is easy access, whilst the disadvantage is dust and careless handling from the passing throng. But it is certainly a simple way to flick through the file names in order to locate the disk you wish to use.

The most popular version of this principle is the all-round 'lazy susan' system, the floppy disk carousel. As many as a hundred disks can be accommodated in this system, and the rotating file is easy to use and economical in terms of space.

At the top of the tree lie the various purpose-built containers for disks which are built for semi-professional purposes. There are cases with suspension racks, used to transport libraries from place to place, there are suspended systems built in the form of trolleys on castors, and there are racks

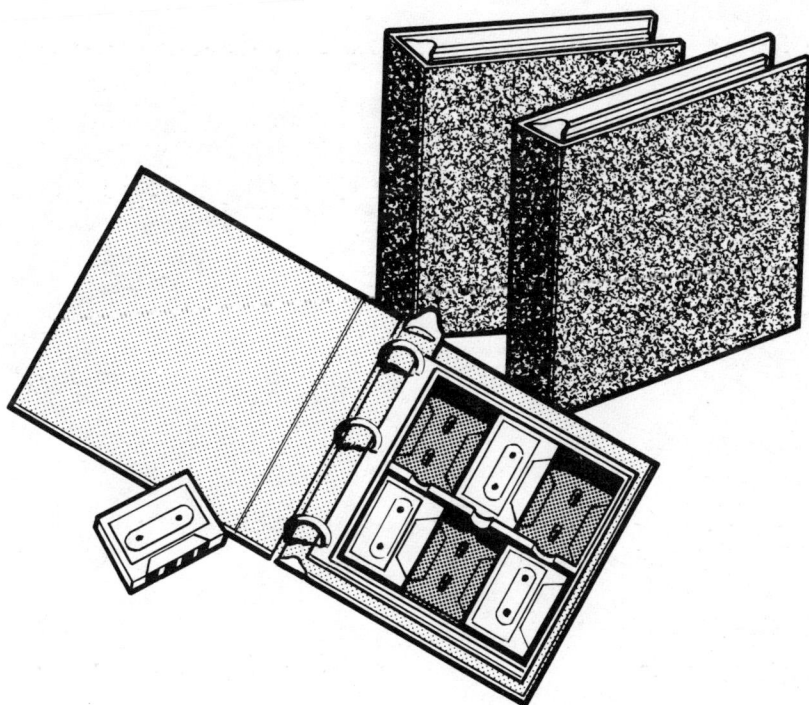

Cassette storage

designed to be locked away in a reinforced cupboard or a safe. For security, these are fairly unbeatable. For cost, they certainly are.

Cassettes are an easier matter. There are many cheap cassette racks available, designed for audio-cassette collections, and perhaps the best of these have locating surfaces which enable them to be fitted together in a rigid stack which grows as the number of cassettes increases. Others are made from metal components and look good, though are inflexible in terms of capacity. Some have been designed primarily for use in cars, and hold the cassettes on a base that can be fixed down permanently, at an angle which makes them easy to select. Some of these might be adaptable for home use.

A small and unobtrusive library of disks or video-cassettes containing favourite TV programmes can always be made to look like books, to stand on a shelf amongst the real thing. Purpose-built holders are available for the video-cassettes, and a modification could be useful for storing games cartridges too.

Some manufacturers are experimenting with other forms of storage. Sinclair, with their QL micro, use a micro-drive not unlike a cross between a cassette deck and a disk drive. This takes tiny matchbox-size cartridges which are slipped into place. As yet these cartridges have not shown themselves to

Sinclair QL microdrive cartridge

be totally reliable. The drives on many computers have been criticised. In particular the QL has a memory that is irritatingly slow to read, according to some specialist users. So ultra-fast memories are now being introduced, and the possibility of using optical memories — which rely on the bi-stability of some minerals, which become transparent or opaque in response to a signal — means that today's memories will seem extremely slow by the end of the century.

Finally, if dust proves to be a major problem, then an air filtration system might be worth investigating. The types now available can filter out minute particles, in some cases smaller than bacteria (though this does not mean you could sensibly rationalise them as a 'health measure' — there are innumerable other ways in which you can come into contact with germs) and their installation need not present too many practical problems. Most of them act by providing positive air-pressure in the environment in which the computer is used, and so this means that considerations of the siting and use of windows and doors should be taken into account.

What extras will I need?

Let us assume that you are toying with the idea of buying a micro-computer for use at home, and possibly to help with the business as well. The micro itself consists of the keyboard, something called a central processing unit (CPU) and the screen (VDU) above or behind it. The question now is: what accessories could you plug in to improve the range of facilities? What *peripherals*, that is.

First in line would be a *cassette deck* to go alongside. This would act as a recorder/player to feed programs into the computer and also to record data that was being stored for filing. In some cases the cassette recorder can be used on its own as a conventional audio tape-recorder, and so it can double up in terms of the functions it offers a family. It may even be that you could connect ('interface') a cassette recorder you already own with the computer you plan to buy. The equipment specialist will be able to advise on that, or the local computer club can find out the answer.

Most micro users become irritated by the time it takes to process information stored in a cassette, and the next most desirable peripheral is the *disk drive*. This sorts out the serious hackers from the merely frivolous dabblers. The floppy disks themselves are inexpensive, and hold a large amount of information out of all proportion to the size of the disk. Indeed, many of the newer small-format diskettes, p. 30, have a capacity much the same as that of the standard floppy disk.

The disk drive itself is a mechanically precise piece of equipment, and naturally not inexpensive. The question of time is therefore the clincher here, and the decision whether to buy a disk drive should sensibly be taken in the light of experience, unless of course you need to invest in one in order to confirm your status as a serious buff.

Disk drive

Much more useful is a *printer*, which can transfer your processed data to a sheet of paper — the so-called hard copy. Some people use a program, like a word-processing system, for example, and then take the refined and polished text in floppy-disk form and print out at work or in the college unit nearby. Others use their machines for calculations, and store the data in a cassette, copying out by hand the figures that emerge at the end.

But the printer is the godsend. It ranges from the inexpensive but low-resolution dot-matrix printers (see p. 37) to highly futuristic versions which may become cheaper as the years go by (p. 39). Perhaps the easiest to justify is the type which can double for use as a conventional typewriter. Indeed you may not need to purchase a printer at all — check first in case your machine can be interfaced with a micro.

Something else you might have at home which could well fit your micro is the video recorder. That can be used to play cassettes of programmes through the micro's VDU, or to play recordings of a higher visual quality and resolution than can be accommodated by the medium-resolution of a conventional television set (p. 21). In this way, a compatible VCR can also become a peripheral.

Games cartridges or 'carts' (p. 69) are amongst the most widely used of accessories. Since they plug into the micro, they are peripherals, by definition,

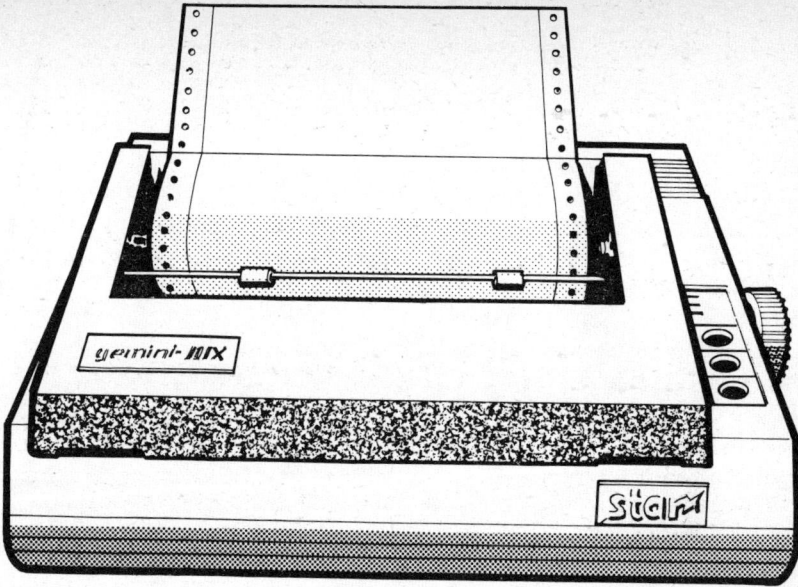

Printer

but do not fit easily into that category as they do not actually perform any function of their own. Incidentally, not all micros can accept carts, and if that is your intention it is as well to check out the point first before deciding on a model.

Control units, to be used in graphics or in selecting data on a two-dimensional display, such as a *joystick*, are useful peripherals. As the handle is moved, a cursor or the position of a selected graphic item can be moved over the VDU until it is in the right position. The same is true if the item is a fighter-plane in a game, whose position has to be carefully and quickly selected to that it can decimate the opposition.

You can also draw directly onto the screen with a *light pen* (explained in more detail on p. 66), which can be extremely useful in computer graphics and in creating designs which you can later store digitally. For many purposes a *graphics tablet* may be a better idea. This takes the form of a complete screen and pen unit, rather like a note-pad in shape and size, on which drawings and diagrams can be set up. Lines drawn with the device are then transferred directly to the screen, and can be stored in a memory for later use.

Some peripherals relate to the conversion of the output into sound, and vice-versa. There is an *acoustic coupler* which enables the output from a computer to be converted into sound tones which can be directly fed via a telephone hand-set into the international telephone network, and thereby transmitted over long distances without any actual wiring connection. Then there are *voice actuators* which interpret a limited range of verbal commands and enable operators to control processes by means of the voice, rather than by having to press anything or turn a switch. This kind of system has great applications for the handicapped, for whom some of the most useful of micro applications have been found.

Lastly, there are graphics display units which can draw out coloured representations of data in a form that is more acceptable to the human subject (like the digital/analog conversion of a clock or watch), and document transmitters which take a printed or drawn original on a piece of paper, and scan it for conversion to telephone-transmissible signals. Virtual simultaneous transmission of passages of typing, signatures, even photographs can be undertaken in this way. However, the transmission of letter-by-letter codes is probably of more daily use than these facsimile transmissions. And since the transmitter is not, strictly speaking, hitched up to your micro (or it needn't be) then it does not count as a true peripheral at all.

In general terms, peripherals are printers, accessory VDUs, and disk drive units. As to the range of accessories, the above outline will have indicated how diverse the present supply can be and, with rapid progress firmly established on all fronts, the range will no doubt mushroom to enormous proportions over the next ten years.

A light pen

An acoustic coupler

Peripherals: the background and some details

Printers

When, inevitably, you find it tedious to note down figures and other items of data from the screen, you will tell yourself you want to have a printer, to provide you with what computer buffs dub *hard copy*.

The earliest form of printer was a mechanical, clattering telex-type terminal. It bounced back and forth, making a noise that could be heard for miles, and producing messy and uneven typing through a worn and fading ribbon (at least this was true of all the versions I came across).

Next on the evolutionary scale was the golf-ball printer, a typewriter with a spherical print head on which were embossed all the characters in the fount (or set of type). The keyboard of a conventional golf-ball typewriter is the traditional QWERTY (or QWERTY-lay) layout. The strange position of the letters is not because of the frequency of use, or anything so everyday and basic. They were set where they still are because of the need to prevent the mechanical arms of the old manual machine from becoming tangled.

The problem with the golf-ball is twofold: firstly its noise (it makes almost as much racket as a manual typewriter, and is just as annoying as a teletext printer), and secondly its speed of operation, which is limited to some 15-16 characters per second. That is fast enough for many applications, and certainly sufficient for daily typewriting use, but not enough for long sheets of hard copy. The standard golf-ball introduced by the IBM company had many

35

ancient precedents (some of the earliest typewriters ever made were fitted with rotating print heads, rather than separate arms) and has been adopted by other golf-ball typewriter manufacturers. The usual golf-ball had an 88-character fount, but some years ago IBM introduced a version with a 96-character fount as a means of up-dating the system (as well as a way round the use of pirate golf-balls by IBM users).

Sadly, the new system seemed to come onto the market at exactly the moment when the golf-ball itself was superseded. In economic terms that cannot have made much sense. The great advantage, though, was the clear type style inherent in the golf-ball principle. There is a similar machine used as a type composer, setting type for offset reproduction by typing onto paper, so good is the clarity of the impression. There is a huge range of symbols available, too, and many manufacturers (notably a firm in Hawaii) produce golf-ball print units with the strangest symbols you could imagine. Nothing else as varied exists to date, though it doubtless will in the future, as more modern printers are introduced.

The successor to the golf-ball was the daisy-wheel. This print-wheel has the letters at the ends of radiating arms from a print wheel that looks like the flowering head from a michaelmas daisy. The letters spin round until the correct character has been selected, and then an impact device shoots forward, imprinting the image of the letter onto the paper. A plastic ribbon is used for this machine, as it was in the golf-ball which preceded it.

This is **bold print.**

This is **shadow print.**

This is **bold and shadow print.**

This is underscore.

This is **shadow and underscore.**

This is super-script.

This is sub-script.

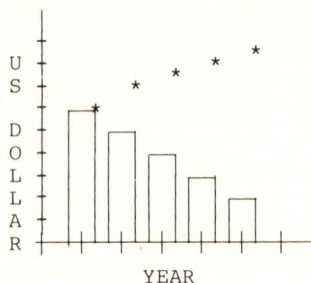

Daisy-wheel printers give clear letter impressions
and can be used for simple graphic printing

The main advantages of the daisy-wheel are that it moves faster than the golf-ball, and is quieter at the same time. The machines themselves are often flimsily made, though, and many have had teething troubles (we used one once which kept spinning round at the most inconvenient moments). But some, notably the Olivetti Praxis system, are useful as lightweight typewriters for conventional purposes, but can also be interfaced with a computer and used as a printer as well (the Praxis is commonly plugged up to the Osborne 1 micro-computer, for example).

A third variation on the theme is the thimble printer. This has an acorn-cup-shaped print unit which spins round to present the right character to the ribbon. These are quite frequently found as computer printers, though they have not been developed as conventional typewriters.

In each case the print unit itself impacts a cast character through a ribbon onto the paper beneath. In the case of the teletype system, it is a case of capital letters only; they are noisy, and slow. The golf-ball is faster but only marginally less noisy, though it does have a huge range of available type styles. The thimble printer is available only for use with computers, and has no part to play as a routine typewriter; whilst the daisy-wheel type is fast, reasonably quiet, but without a wide range of styles. That is changing almost by the day, however; and by the time this book is beginning to lose its pages the range may well be larger.

There is a further type of impact printer which has no pre-formed letters at all, but which makes them up as it goes along. This is the dot-matrix device. The system works by making letters up from separate dots in this way:

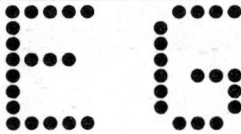

But there are limitations to the early matrix printers (the example above being made up from an array of dots five by eight in number). For example, there were no true descenders: letters like g or y had the 'tails' represented by short versions which did not truly descend below the line and the level of the other letters, like o and s, as they should.

Matrix printers improved somewhat when they went to a higher resolution standard of nine by seven. But more recently the sights have been set higher again. A new type which has been made available in a portable typewriter capable of being interfaced with a computer has a matrix made up of 24 x 18 dots. The resulting print quality (with 24 x 18 = 432 separate dot positions to choose for each character) is so high that it is very close to the results you would expect of a golf-ball type-head.

The practical difficulty of the matrix printer is that there is no standard code for the way impulses are interpreted. For this reason it is essential to find out beforehand whether the printer you have in mind is suitable for interfacing with your chosen micro. The Brother EP-44 matrix printer, for instance, which came on the market in 1984, has a built-in RS—232C interface (p. 47). This has 25 pin connections, which provide two channels for the transmission of data. The RS—232 standard was laid down by the

May 10, 1984

John Smith
The Important Company
1111 N. Broadway
Chicago, IL 60640

Dear John,

It was a pleasure to have breakfast with you Monday morning.
It gave me a better understanding of what we are trying to
accomplish. I hope that you view Video Etc. as a full line
computer products supplier.

Attached you will find the revised proposal. This reflects
the substitution of the **Smith-Corona D200** printer. This
harware proposal represents a substantial savings for your
network members. Coupled with Len's program they will have
a unique opportunity to effectively join the computer
revolution.

If you have any questions, please feel free to call me.

Sincerely,

Bill Gehl
Business Markets Manager
VIDEO ETC.
465 Lake Cook Road
Deerfield, IL 60015
(312) 498-9669

*A dot-matrix printer which could be used for correspondence. The individual
dots give an uneven look, inferior to conventional typewriters — but the
speed of printing is high even if the spelling ('harware') is none too reliable*

Electronics Industry Association as a specification for interconnections
between peripherals in telecommunications. The Brother EP−44 should
therefore be interconnectable with equipment conforming to the same
specifications. Another 24-column matrix printer is the Epson HX−20,
which the manufacturers claim will run for fifty hours on its own internal
(rechargeable) batteries. This acts as a micro-computer with a 16K memory,
but does not take a full-sized paper. The EP−44, on the other hand, takes
full-sized A4 paper and can double as a portable typewriter for letters, scripts
and memoranda.
    The main advantage of the matrix printer, if you look to the future, is that
the combination of dots can be triggered to produce an endless assortment

of characters, depending on the memory supplied with the machine. Greek letters, scientific symbols, even a change from roman to italic printing would not require the use of any replacement print head. All that would be necessary would be a different program to encode the new characters, and from then on the typewriter would do the rest. My own view is that some version of the dot matrix principle will be the future for home-use printers, and that the daisy-wheel, and all other petal printers will be obsolescent within a decade.

Printers: the way ahead

The very first methods of printing relied on the pressing of a character onto a piece of paper, and in some form that has remained the principle ever since. Typewriters involved the impact of a character which imprinted ink from a ribbon, instead of ink from the character's surface, but the idea of contact with the surface remained. Golf-ball and petal printers, and even the most up-to-the-minute dot matrix printers, are all variations on the impact principle. The new generation of printers abandons that concept altogether.

A system which has already been adopted for use in printing calculators is the thermal printer. Here the roll of paper is coated with a thick layer of the 'ink', and this in turn is covered with a fine film of aluminium. A set of print wires is used to form characters on a dot-matrix basis, but instead of impacting the paper an electric charge is applied for a fraction of a second, heating up the point at which the wire touches the aluminium surface and burning it away, revealing the 'ink' beneath.

These thermal printers are silent in operation, but make demands on the batteries powering the unit. A major disadvantage is the cost of the paper rolls which, because of their complex manufacturing requirements, are amongst the most expensive forms of paper available. But the printers are relatively cheap to make, and they are extremely fast.

An intriguing, newer version of a non-impact printer is the ink-jet system. As the name says, these work by ejecting a spray of ink onto the paper without any physical contact being otherwise made. The concept itself is simple enough. The technical problems lie in controlling the direction of the jet. It was apparent, early on, that the direction of the jet itself was not something which could be easily controlled. Jets are relatively heavy, and there would be such practical difficulties in moving it up and down and from side to side that a high-speed printer would be out of the question.

The modern ink-jet printer works not by moving the jet itself, but by controlling the ink spray once it has been ejected. The jet itself produces a mist of ink droplets, and as they leave the nozzle they are given a static electrical charge. Metal plates on either side of the emerging jet carry a charge as well, and by altering this the droplets of ink can be attracted or repelled and so set on course for the paper surface in exactly the correct trajectory, so printing a character of the desired kind. In practice the jet is switched on and off at predetermined intervals, and the jet is directed up and down as the printer moves along, so elaborating the desired character. The translation of the input into the movement and interruption of the jet droplets is undertaken by a ROM unit built into the printer.

The nearest approach to a low-cost ink-jet printer was the Olivetti JP–101, which was launched with a range of interfaces for many commonly-used computers (including the RS–232 and Centronics systems). As demand increases and the development and tooling-up costs are recovered, the price of peripherals like this will fall. A long-term advantage of the system is that there is no limit to the range of symbols and characters that the printer could produce. A new set of instructions from a different ROM would provide the means of printing foreign alphabets, scientific symbols, trade abbreviations, and even unusual type-faces, as in the case of matrix printers.

Electrical charges are used to control the ink in a different kind of non-impact printer based on the same principle as the xerographic photocopier. The print function operates by means of the transfer of particles of toner, as the ink is called, to the surface of the paper, by means of electrical charges. A line of print needles is used to pick up the fine powder and release it onto the paper which moves beneath. In the types available, the toner is then fused to the paper surface by means of passage over a heated roller. This melts the plastic component of the toner so that it flows into the paper and sets, just like an instant-drying ink.

The V–80 electrostatic printer can print a line of type in one-sixteenth of a second, and the needle array gives a resolution of 200 points per inch (40,000 per square inch or 6,000 per square centimetre). ROM modules have been provided for a range of different alphabets and several type styles. This is a very expensive machine at present, but it could be foreseen as the progenitor of desk-top versions for home use within a decade.

In terms of quality, however, it is the laser printer which is in the Rolls-Royce class (in terms of cost, equally). The laser can be modified instantaneously, since there is no 'inertia' in the beam itself and the mirrors which are used to direct the laser beam are instantly responsive. In use, the laser scans across a rotating print drum and builds up the character by being directed and switched on and off until the requisite regions of the drum have been left with an electrostatic charge. Onto the drum toner is attracted, and the printing itself then proceeds in much the same way as a conventional xerographic copier.

The advantage of the laser system is its rapidity. Industrial equipment using powerful gas lasers are being used to generate hard copy at up to four *pages* every second. Laser diodes are now being developed for use in laser printers which would have a print speed of four seconds per page. These are not yet available for home use, and would seem to fulfil a high-throughput demand more typical of commercial applications. But time will tell.

Attention is also being paid to magnetic printers, which rely on the attraction of toner particles through a magnetic field rather than by an

40

electrostatic charge, and ion printers in which the electrically-charged particles are ions — charged forms of atoms.

Plotters

Whether you need a plotter depends on your requirement for graphic or pictorial printout. Plotters trace instructions in the vertical and horizontal axes, x and y, and place a drawing instrument at the indicated position, moving it relative to the paper (or vice-versa) until the drawing is complete. They are often used to print graphs and histograms, but can be used to make analog data out of digital material (which as we know makes them easier to interpret) or even to draw a picture. They have been known as $x—y$ plotters, graphical plotters, digital plotters or incremental plotters. But plotters will do.

The most useful task which plotters perform is to provide hard copies of graphical printout, so that in that sense a plotter is the pictorial equivalent of a printer. Printers can produce graphical material by the use of regular symbols, but the plotter is the only real answer to reproducing graphics.

Up-market plotters are available with several coloured pens which are used to build up complex graphs and could, doubtless, make some very fine artwork if that was the intention. Others work rapidly over paper passing round a roller. Some are small units, suitable for the personal businessman, whilst others use a range of colours and have a resolution down to a thousandth of an inch.

Papers: choosing for your printer

For many purposes you can use the same kind of paper for your printer as you might use for your office. Normal A4 bond paper, which you may find at a discount in a stationer's (many of whom handle bankrupt or out-of-date stock), can be extremely cheap, compared with the branded computer papers a dealer might hope to sell to you.

But that is only where one-off copies are required. Some printers require coated papers with a defined surface, and here you may find that inferior versions are still dusty with the coating which is used to give the paper its print quality. Dust is no friend of machine, nor of mankind; and wear can result on the former, if not so much on the latter.

For business or professional use you may wish to keep a simultaneous copy. Here you have two choices, either the NCR-type papers (the initials standing for No Carbon Required) — the other NCR you have seen designates the National Cash Register company, incidentally — which produce a blueish copy, and smell faintly of chemicals; or you can use OTC paper (One-Time Carbon) which comes interleaved with a thin form of carbon-paper. This is pulled out and thrown away after use.

The advantage is that you can have your own name and address or company logo printed on stationery for computers easily enough, and still keep a carbon copy for your files. But it is imperative to check that the weights of the papers you select match those preferred by your printer. For most purposes an acceptable paper is between 50 and 70 grams per square metre (gsm).

There is a form of paper that comes fan-folded in a continuous length, ready to go straight into the machine. Its principal advantage is that it does not need to be fed by hand, one sheet at a time, and so it is vital if you are going to handle thousands of accounts at a time. Paper of the NCR or OTC type is readily available in this format, and overprinting is possible. However, bear in mind that you can program your own equipment to print (in a different type-face, if you are using a non-impact or matrix system) a letterhead at the top of each sheet, which would obviate the cost of commercial stationery printing.

Much of this paper comes perforated according to standard formats, but when reading the specifications you should bear in mind that:

· the *pitch* of the sprocket holes is the distance between the *centre* of each hole (or the top of two adjacent holes); it is the spacing *of* the holes, and not the spacing *between* them;

· the *width* of the paper may refer to the area available for printing, i.e. inside the lines of sprocket holes; it is not always the overall width of the entire roll *including* the margins (which can be removed) in which the sprocket-holes are found;

· in terms of folded forms, the *pitch* refers to the distance between each join, or each fold;

· when printing self-adhesive labels supplied in long rolls on release paper, the *width* and *depth* describe the length and height of each label respectively, and the *horizontal spacing* means the distance between each label. Here, of course, the pitch would refer to the separation of the tops of adjacent labels. It should not be confused with the depth.

It should be emphasised that most computer paper (at around 60 gsm) is lighter than the kind of high-quality paper that is ordinarily used for business or domestic letter-head (say, 80 gsm). The kind of result you want to obtain should be borne in mind when you choose a printing system. The production of computer-originated letters on stationery that was lightweight and inferior to the feel would be counter-productive, no matter how exciting it all seemed at the time.

Producing graphics

Graphics can be produced on any micro. But what kind of graphics, and of what kind of quality? It has been known for decades that you can make up pictures and patterns on a manual typewriter easily enough, and low-resolution pictures have been transmitted down teleprinter lines by building up an image from the range of symbols available on the keyboard.

If you use a VDU with a raster for graphic work* then the slanting or sloping lines are made up of stepped straight, horizontal lines. Close inspection shows that the wavy lines you think you see are actually made up of zig-zag components of the horizontal raster. Other VDUs are built on a different principle, and are designated *vector display generators*. They actually produce a wavy line, rather than simply trying to generate an impression of one.

First Quarter Sales

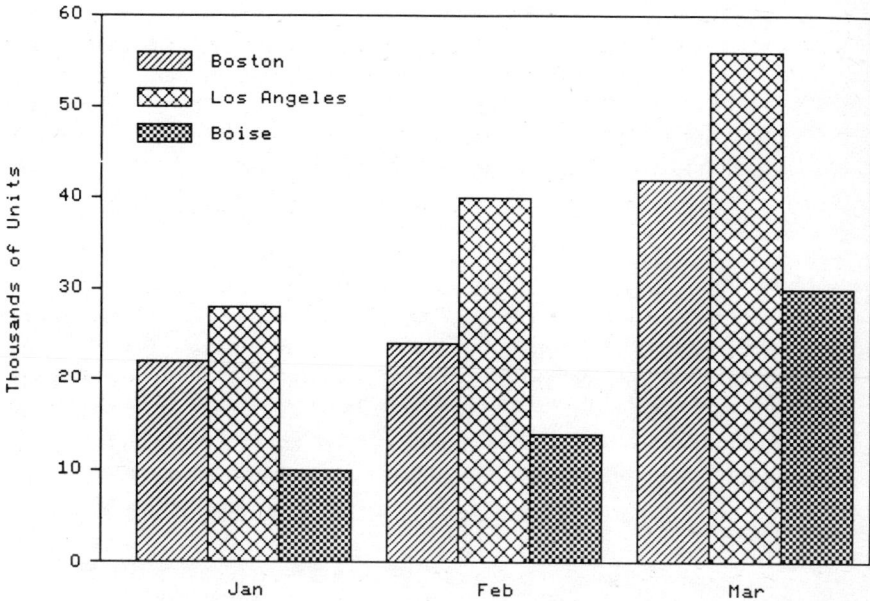

Graphics printed on a LaserJet printer marketed by Hewlett-Packard. Here the matrix is effectively used to generate histogram displays

Low-resolution graphics are easily exemplified by the artwork used to illustrate television-based information systems like Prestel. In this case the screen is divided up into 960 locations which can be divided up into six blocks, each of which can be separately programmed. But a screen of this type, made up of 24 x 40 discrete (separate) packets of information, gives only a poor picture quality. Any oblique or curved line on the Prestel display can be clearly seen to be produced by a series of stepped boxes. But then Prestel is not meant for pictorial displays. That's what the television programmes are there for. The coloured graphics are only there to amuse, and to produce a visually interesting background. In essence, rather than

*The raster is the pattern of lines on the screen, produced by its being constantly scanned by a moving spot. Rasters have nothing to do with Jamaican lifestyles.

displaying a character on each of the screen locations, such as A or B or 5, it prints out the whole character area as a rectangle, thus ■, and uses combinations of those to generate the patterns you see.

It is usual to think in terms of these discrete picture-forming units when considering any graphics problem: they are normally known as *pixels*. The greater the number of pixels on the screen, the higher the resolution of the picture you generate. Images of very low resolution have been used for some time as the inspiration for a series of eye-catching advertisement posters, which look like nothing but coloured squares when viewed from close by, but which merge into an acceptable view of some easily-recognised scene when looked at from a distance. Each of the coloured squares can be thought of as a pixel, in this sense. Displays in which there are easily-visible pixels on the VDU are known as *chunky graphics*. These are typical of the small, 16K-memory computers, but plug-in expansion units can be obtained to upgrade the display and produce smooth and flowing outlines by increasing the resolution through a decrease in pixel size.

The ultimate resolution is obtained by dot-sized pixels, and this is the system you would need to adopt if you intended to try any three-dimensional graphics. This sounds like a contradiction in terms (how could you produce a 3-D image on a two-dimensional screen?) and of course it is not true three-dimensional plotting we are talking about. That may come later!

Displays of 3-D graphics produce an image of a solid-looking object which can then be turned round, as it were, on the screen and inspected from different angles. (The 1982 Walt Disney Production of TRON featured the adventures of human characters trapped in a world generated by computer graphics, and it is certainly a film to see, if you want to study how high-resolution graphics can be made to work.)

Can truly three-dimensional displays be generated? There are three promising approaches at present:

The red green image (anaglyph) system

This is the principle on which the early 3-D cinema films were based. The picture is produced in the form of two overlapping images, one of them red in colour (and representing the view of the right eye) and the other green (representing the view of the left eye). Lightweight spectacles are worn during viewing, so that there is a green filter over the left eye and a red one over the right. This system keeps the inappropriate image out of the wrong eye, and allows each eye to receive the image intended for it. The result is the visualisation of a fairly good 3-D image. As the picture itself is not too bright in terms of light intensity, the eye relies mostly on the rod cells in the retina for vision, rather than the cone cells. It is the rods which are concerned with intensity, rather than colour, and so the image is seen reasonably clearly. The fact that one eye is seeing in red whilst the other is seeing in green is largely ignored by the brain.

A version of this has also been used to transmit 3-D television programmes.

Here two overlapping images were generated, corresponding to the view seen by the two eyes, and the problem lay in the fact that the image when viewed *without* special glasses was indistinct. It is part of the regulations governing TV transmission in Britain that picture quality must be high, and there were complaints on that score. Even so the effect of solidity, when the first experimental programmes were transmitted in 1983, was reasonably impressive and there may be something in this idea for the future.

The polarised projector system

In this variation on the theme, the overlapping images are produced in real colour, but are projected through filters which polarise the light beam. The images corresponding to the views of the separate eyes are projected into the screen so that the polarisation plane between the two was separated by 90°. The polarising filters were set at right angles to each other and at 45° to the vertical.

Spectacles were provided to separate out the images, but this time instead of being of different colours they were made of polarising filters once more set at 45° to each other, but this time at 90° to the polarisation of the image destined for the other eye. The result was that the separate eyes received their separated images, and a vivid impression of 3-D in full colour was the result.*

The first popular film to be released in this format was *Jaws 3* and some of the scenes in which portions of victims floated out towards the audience, and a frog leapt into your lap, were well worth seeing for the novelty of the process. At present there is no way in which a home VDU with such a 3-D capacity could be produced, but research into the idea is progressing. Certainly it is possible to make red/green 3-D graphics on a home computer that was capable of the picture quality required.

The 3-D helix

This device has been produced in prototype form by the laboratories in the

---

*This is not the place to go into the details of polarising filters. Polarised light is formed by altering the plane of vibrations in a light beam so that instead of taking up a random pattern, with vibrations in all directions, they are more or less in the same direction (say, vertical). Viewed through a vertically oriented filter, such a beam of light would appear much as normal. But as the filter was rotated through 90° the intensity would begin to drop, only slightly at first, until when the filter was exactly at 90° the light would be cut off almost entirely. Polarised sunglasses are made on this principle. To demonstrate it, take two pairs of sunglasses out of the rack and hold them at arm's length. Then place one of the lenses behind another, and whilst holding one of them still slowly rotate the other one around, like tuning a dial. The moment of extinction comes when the view through the combined glasses changes from being normal to suddenly disappearing to darkness altogether. At this stage, the filters in the two glasses are at 90° to each other. That shows how the polarised images are kept separate in 3-D films of this type. The reason why polarising sunglasses are popular is because most reflections are polarised, and this kind of accessory cuts out the glare of reflections almost totally, without over-darkening the rest of the view.

University of Heidelberg in West Germany. It is still very new (indeed at the time I saw it demonstrated, the company who funded the research — IBM — did not even know it was working) but it is also extremely simple.

The principle relies on a spiral of plastic — a helix — which spins round too fast to be seen by the human eye. Somewhere around 30 cycles per second would be sufficient. Onto this turning shape, a spot of laser light is shone, its exact position being determined by a sensitive mirror. The mirror can be controlled by a micro-computer, so that the spot moves from side to side. The secret is to coordinate the movement of the spot of light with the turning of the helix, a relatively simple task. As the spot moves about, it builds up a three-dimensional representation, which seems to hover in the air since the plastic helix is turning too fast to be seen. In a darkened room a solid-looking image can be generated, and it is true 3-D in the sense that you can walk around it and inspect it from all points of the compass. In that respect, this is a truer form of 3-D image generation than the flat-screen versions described in the previous two sections.

This could clearly apply to home use. Indeed it would not be absolutely necessary to use a laser beam at all, for a single light beam of a more conventional kind could be used instead. You would need a rotating helix of the kind shown, controlled by a unit which was related to the position of the mirror; and you could even envisage a system in which the light was modulated through filters, or even that there were several beams of coloured light, building up a full-blown, full-colour, lifelike representation of a solid form. Nothing of this sort is available, nor is it foreseeable at present. But there should be the germ of an idea here which an enterprising hacker could work up into a functioning system.

Otherwise the need for graphics should be considered before you embark on establishing a micro set-up for yourself, and it is as always important to investigate the software options that could provide you with the facilities you require.

The best and most easily available example of good quality graphics must be the Atari series, produced in Japan. The trade-name apparently derives from the Japanese word used in the board-game *wei-ch'i* (Go) to mean impending defeat, or a challenge (like calling 'check' in chess, perhaps). But the range of games they have produced is without equal and the graphics are an object lesson for home programmers. Their most famous game was Pac-Man, which earned around $200m per year before versions of it were dreamed up by other software manufacturers.

One of the most interesting graphic systems in recent new computers is the Macintosh software which allows easy 'editing' of displayed graphics. This could be a sample of systems that will become commonplace in design studios within a few years.

The RS-232 *serial interface*

This multi-pin plug was developed for use between certain computers and peripherals, and between computers and telephone networks, but it has become semi-standard in much of the industry. It has two rows of connecting pin positions, a top row of thirteeen and a lower row of twelve. They are numbered 1-25 from left to right, upper row first. Data is transmitted on one pin and received on another. The ten generally-used standard positions are as follows.

Pin Number:	Signal:
1	Protective earth
2	Transmitted data
3	Received data
4	Request to send
5	Clear to send
6	Data set ready
7	Signal earth
8	Carrier detect
20	Terminal ready
22	Ring Indicator

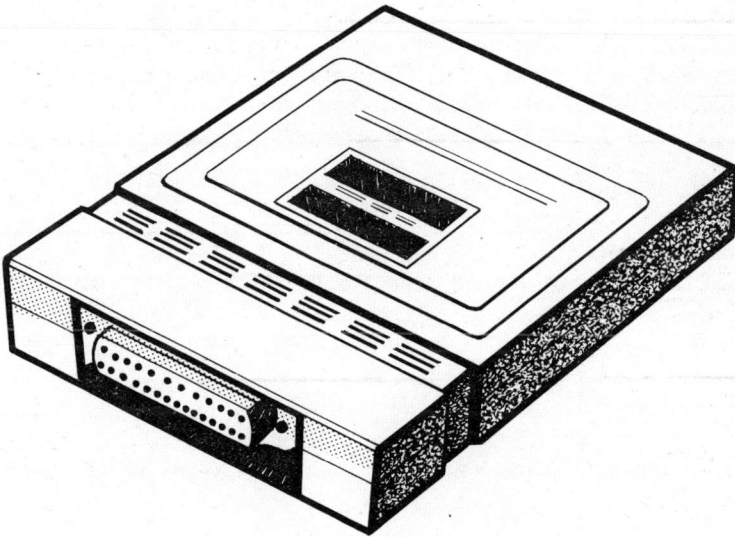

An RS232 serial interface

What about word processors?

Many users find them indispensable. I tried working with one for a while, but found that I preferred to process words in my mind rather than tinker with

47

them on a VDU. One of the main disadvantages was summed up in advice given by an early advocate of the idea: 'Prepare yourself for a five-fold increase in the amount of paper you consume,' he said. He was right.

The earliest type — which are still found — lacked a screen as such, but featured text-storage on tape which was controlled and printed out through a conventional typewriter. Many modern varieties of word processor utilise a small display which shows a few words or perhaps a line of text at a time.

More recently have arisen the word-processing software packages that can be used with a regular micro-computer and these, particularly if you have your own letter-quality printer or a typewriter which can interface with your equipment, are useful in many ways. You can enter text, amend it, sort out specific words or phrases within it, correct its spelling and generally tart it up until you are completely satisfied. At the end of that time you can press a button and it will all spill out as fast as your printer can carry it.

Anybody who wants to have a perfect printout on a typewriter and cannot obtain it any other way will find a word processor invaluable. Authors, in the main, do not necessarily need word processors since their text is always set in type. So an author can make the kind of small changes that most of them would perform on a WP system, using pencil marks on the original manuscript. By the time it is set in type, the changes are all incorporated, and the reader certainly never sees how clean, or how heavily edited, the original might have been.

One excellent use for them is the printing of a repeated letter to a large number of people. The names and addresses can be called up from a memory and inserted at the right place in the letters, all without the need for human intervention. It is a great time- and manpower-saver. Most people must have received those personalised letters which say something like this:

YES MRS McCARTHY, YOU TOO COULD HAVE A GLEAMING NEW PORSCHE STANDING OUTSIDE No. 36 GRANGE AVENUE DOWN THERE IN DOGSTHORPE. . . .

These are, of course, done on such a system — frequently very tattily. But real problems only arise when the data is transposed by a clerk so that you end up with:

YES MRS PORSCHE, YOU TOO COULD HAVE A GLEAMING NEW DOGSTHORPE STANDING OUTSIDE No. 36 McCARTHY AVENUE

and that (or something very like it) has happened many times.

Why do I get uncomfortable using a computer at home?

Either because you are not used to it, or because the set-up is wrong. There have been some examinations of this complicated problem, and in Europe there are some enforceable codes of practice which apply to the use of desk-top computers.

In Germany, for instance, the recommendations cover the following points:

Screen displays should avoid excessive stress and strain, preferably dark letters against a light background (the opposite of the normal screen where luminous lime-green letters appear against a black background), fitted with a filter to avoid reflections from the screen (the problem we have already encountered with ordinary television screens). The brilliance of the screen should be adequate in comparison with the lighting in the room as a whole; letters in the format on the screen should not be distorted, which would make interpretation a strain; the screen should be as large as possible, so that information is not compressed; and the preferred colours are orange, yellow or green.

Positioning is facilitated if the screen is adjustable in height, easily readable at 50 cms, and oriented so that the user does not have to look up or down more than 35°.

Keyboards should not be too compact, for this causes cramping of movements and strain. A separate keyboard is preferred, and the angle of the surface should be less than 25°.

Texts and holders should be clear (bad handwriting to be avoided); glossy folders or shiny paper should be avoided (again because of the reflection problem), and text holders should be set at 15°-17° from horizontal.

Tables and chairs should conform to the following rules: plenty of space for them, adjustable and/or rotating chairs preferred; desk or table surfaces should be matt or semi-matt to cut glare; minimum table top area should be 120 cms x 120 cms, recommended height 72 cms with at least 60 cms of leg-room.

Eye tests are recommended for operators on recruitment and thereafter every five years to age forty-five; from then on a three-yearly test is advised.

You might think that this is all part of German bureaucracy. Not so. The Swedish regulations, I find, are distinctly more dictatorial in tone. Their National Board of Occupational Safety has published a directive on the reading of display screens which gives the following 'rules for operation':

1. Ambient lighting must be suitably adapted. Special importance must be attached to lighting conditions at work places where reading of display screens occurs regularly. Generally the illumination required is lower than in ordinary office work. In work places where work is conducted continuously at display screens, an illumination of between 200 and 300 lux may be suitable.

Note: Lower levels of illumination may be appropriate in certain working environments of a specialised nature (e.g. monitoring and traffic control).

2. When ambient lighting is subdued (as per point No. 1), supplementary lighting must be provided for other working areas near the display screen. Supplementary lighting must be adjustable and fitted with glare control arrangements.

3. Excessive differences of illumination in the field of vision produce what is termed contrast glare. The work place should therefore be organised in such a way that the background to the display does not include a window or any other glaring light source. Bright reflections in the display screen are to be avoided.

4. The visual distance to the display screen and the angle of inclination of the display screen should be individually adjustable with due regard being paid to other ergonomic* requirements. In the case of employees who wear spectacles, it is important that the optical correction is well adapted to the visual distance, or vice-versa.

Note: Ordinary spectacles for private use are often unadapted to the visual distance occurring in display screen work. Traditional bifocal lenses are unsuitable in many cases, because they often entail a strenuous work posture when used for display screen reading.

5. If an employee has a refractive error and incurs visual discomfort in connection with display screen work when using spectacles intended for normal purposes, the display screen must be moved to a position where the discomfort is eliminated. If this is not possible, the employer is to provide the employee with special spectacles which have been tested for display screen work.

6. If eye fatigue or visual discomfort tend to develop, the work must be organised in such a way that the employee can intermittently be given periods of rest or work involving more conventional visual requirements.

No doubt that when the Common Market gets hold of the possibilities, there will be countless more regulations to deal with. The serious point behind these controls is that working with a display screen or VDU is not an ordinary, relaxing, easy, simple business. Eye-strain can result because the experience is not one we are accustomed to. Muscles can become tense, and obsessive users of micros at home can suffer from the tensions that result at an emotional level. As the German and Swedish regulations illustrate forcibly, much care and attention must be paid to making the computer environment suitable for the user. It must never be the other way round.

*Ergonomics is the study of adapting the design of machines to the anatomical requirements of human beings.

Could I make my own micro-computer?

Plenty of enthusiasts do. The way to accomplish this is to invest in a kit. The process of putting it together will help teach a good deal about the way a computer functions. However, building a computer from a kit is not a suitable task for the novice. Unless you are used to electrical work (precision soldering in particular) it would be foolhardy to start like this, at the top end. You should have made your own radio set or an amplifier before embarking on an ambitious project of this kind.

Before buying a kit it is important to make sure that the completed version will be able to perform the range of tasks you have in mind for it. The questions on p. 17 are just as relevant here.

It is equally important to make sure that you have the time and patience. A typical computer kit may involve up to a thousand soldering operations, each of them precise and skilful manouevres. The other person who may need time and perseverance is the man who sold you the kit. In the event of problems, he is the individual who should be ready to advise and assist, so it helps to know by local enquiries that he is likely to be able to do this, and what's more is able to do it properly.

Finally, make sure you are well equipped before you start. The correct solder is important (older cored solders contain corrosive compounds which can etch through a joint after it has been carefully made), and it helps to have proper cable-strippers rather than relying on your teeth or an old penknife. An accurate multimeter is invaluable, as there is no better way to test for short-circuits or high-resistance junctions.

The only other word of advice I would offer is to see if you can obtain a stand-mounted magnifying glass, or even a binocular low-power microscope (Russian industrial microscopes can still be found at a reasonable price). Not only will they help you assemble tiny components and solder them into position neatly, but they are handy for finding droplets of solder that have escaped and made their way into a compromising position. A fine pair of forceps or tweezers can help too.

4 Mere Technicalities

What do today's computers do?

Computers are more than calculators. The first thing a computer can do is, certainly, to calculate; but they do more besides. They can *store information* by encoding specific items of data in a memory. The memory may be permanent, it may be temporary; you may be able to alter it, you may not. But the storage of information that the computer itself generates as it *processes information* fed in by the user is an important part of its work.

Computers can *control*. They can be hooked up to a system and regulate it minutely, whether it is a robot in a car factory or toast grilling in your kitchen. And they can *communicate*, often via phone lines. In this way a computer can have access to information held by another one, often a considerable distance away; and information from a range of sources can usefully be brought together. Once a computer system has been set up, it is remarkable how useful it can be. Many of us have booked holidays through the use of a computer terminal at a travel agent's. And how did we ever manage to make airline bookings without computer terminals?

How do computers handle information?

By making it simpler. They used to call computers 'electronic brains', but that is a bad term and it is just as well it has fallen into disrepute. Computers are not brainy at all. They are electronic morons. A computer would multiply 17 x 31 by doing seventeen, or thirty-one, addition sums. It would multiply 3 x 2 by performing additions. If a youngster did that, you would consider him mathematically illiterate, or just plain stupid. So is a computer. It can only do what it is told.

But it does it at very high speed. That is why the lengthy version of a comparatively simple problem — like 17 x 31 — can be successfully performed by a computer. It does it in the smallest fraction of a second, and still comes up with the answer sooner than you can. So computers are stupid, but fast. That is a point worth emphasising.

The way information is handled by a computer fits very well into this concept. The computer is too stupid to handle discrete items of information like 'seventeen' or 'thirty-one'. Every item which it assimilates has to be reduced to a combination of no more than two symbols: a choice between on and off, the difference between a light switch which is flicked on and then off. There are no in-betweens. The computer is built to handle highly complicated combinations of on and off, in numerical terms 0 and 1. That is how, using the example of binary numbering, each piece of information can be encoded in terms of simple electrical signals which are combinations of 'on' and 'off'. Each of the 0 or 1 alternatives is known as a *bit* of information. A group of them (traditionally eight) forms a single computer-word known as a *byte*. The word thirty-one, for instance, would correspond to two bytes, and in the computer's code (what is called machine code) would be 0110011 0110001 (see the accompanying tables). That is an eye-full for us, doubtless; but to the fast computer it is easily handled. The code for 3 and 1 which I have cited here is the standard code known as ASCII (American Standard Code for Information Interchange), and it uses a combination of 0 and 1 to represent the characters on a keyboard, starting with 1000001 (meaning 'A') and ending with 1111111 (symbolizing 'rubout').

Character	ASCII code	Character	ASCII code
A	1000001	[	1011011
B	1000010	\	1011100
C	1000011	]	1011101
D	1000100	↑	1011110
E	1000101	←	1011111
F	1000110	!	0100001
G	1000111	"	0100010
H	1001000	#	0100011
I	1001001	$	0100100
J	1001010	%	0100101
K	1001011	&	0100110
L	1001100	'	0100111
M	1001101	(	0101000
N	1001110	)	0101001
O	1001111	*	0101010
P	1010000	+	0101011
Q	1010001	,	0101100
R	1010010	−	0101101
S	1010011	.	0101110
T	1010100	/	0101111
U	1010101	0	0110000
V	1010110	1	0110001
W	1010111	2	0110010

X	1011000	3	0110011
Y	1011001	4	0110100
Z	1011010	5	0110101
@	1000000	6	0110110
		7	0110111
		8	0111000
		9	0111001
		:	0111010
		;	0111011
		<	0111100
		>	0111110
		=	0111101
		?	0111111

ASCII control codes

Code	Abbreviation	Instruction
0000000	NUL	Null
0000001	SOH	Start of Heading
0000010	STX	Start of Text
0000011	ETX	End of Text
0000100	EOT	End of Transmission
0000101	ENQ	Enquiry
0000110	ACK	Acknowledge
0000111	BEL	Bell
0001000	BS	Back Space
0001001	HT	Horizontal Tabulation
0001010	LF	Line Feed
0001011	VT	Vertical Tabulation
0001100	FF	Form Feed
0001101	CR	Carriage Return
0001110	SO	Shift control Out
0001111	SI	Shift control In
0001000	DLE	Data Link Escape
0010001	DC1	Device Control 1
0010010	DC2	Device Control 2
0010011	DC3	Device Control 3
0010100	DC4	Device Control 4
0010101	NAK	Negative Acknowledgement
0010110	SYN	Synchronous Idle
0010111	ETB	End Transmission Block
0011000	CAN	Cancel
0011001	EM	End of Medium

0011010	SUB	Substitute
0011011	ESC	Escape
0011100	FS	File Separator
0011110	RS	Record Separator
0011111	US	Unit Separator
0100000	SP	Space
1111111	DEL	Delete, rubout

Table of the ASCII codes used by many computers

The user does not have to know anything of the above codes in everyday computing, of course, since they are what the device uses in its internal processes. An idea of the complexity involved for the (intelligent but slow) human brain can be experienced by working out a coded sentence such as this one:

```
1001001 0100000 1010100 1010010 1010101 1010011 1010100
0100000 1011001 1001111 1010101 0100000 1001111 1010111
1001110 0100000 0110001 0110000 0110001 0100000 1001110
1001111 1010011 0110001 0100110 0110010 0100001
```

The solution would be apparent to a (dull but fast) computer in the time it took to type it out.

There is a clever and vitally important safeguard built into code systems like the ASCII version. Code systems rely on a complex series of 0 and 1 signals which have to be read correctly. If they are not, a single word or a number could throw the entire transmission out of line. A moment of electrical interference, for instance, could be picked up as a 1 when a 0 was intended; conversely a momentary failure to transmit a 1 would be recorded as an 0. As can be imagined, the consequences of such a misreading would be severe. Try altering a 1 or a 0 in each line of the coded message and see what you end up with.

So the eighth bit in each byte is designated as a 'parity bit'. This is why the actual number of bits in each byte is seven, and not eight, as you will have noticed. The idea is very simple: if there is an *even* number of 1s in the encoded signal, then the parity bit is 1, whereas if there is an odd number of 1s the parity bit is a 0. The receiving device checks the digits as they are fed in, and compares the total number with the parity bit. If there was, say, a parity bit of 1 when there was actually an *odd* number of 1s in the character, then clearly the byte would contain an error. A signal to that effect can be generated, so that the error is identified before any unwanted consequences occur.

Need I master machine code?

No. Machine codes are specific for the computer for which they were designed, and are not readily interchangeable. Most domestic micros are intended to use more literary languages, like BASIC, and these are more than sufficient for any purpose other than one for which you would need special training. On the other hand, many amateurs are now enjoying the challenge of teaching themselves machine code.

Where did BASIC get its name?

Not from where you might think. It is a crafted acronym, and stands for Beginner's All-purpose Symbolic Instruction Code, though it is no longer just a beginner's language but one of the most widely used commercial languages.

What exactly is a CPU?

The initials designate the *central processing unit* of your computer. This is the hub of the activity, where all the main computing is carried out.

A CPU is usually a single pre-packaged unit carrying microchips, and all the connecting circuitry. These days a CPU may contain a single chip which can control the computer's functions, carry out the data-processing, and transmit data between the various inputs, outputs and memory centres. This is the *microprocessor*.

Each CPU has several components. The most important is the *arithmetic-logic unit*, or a.l.u., which is used for carrying out mathematical and logical computations. Associated with this central system are a number of registers, which are sites where information can be stored whether these are input data, items arising during the work of the a.l.u., or control functions.

Then there has to be a control unit which can recall data from a memory, using an address decoder; translate and implement instructions from a program; synchronise the activities of the program in strict sequence, and send output signals which trigger the rest of the computer's components (indicator lamps and so on).

The CPU would be the 'brain' of the computer, if a computer had a brain, which it hasn't.

What does 'K' mean?

The expression K arose in the conventional scientific symbol for a thousand. Thus a thousand metres is a kilometre (km) and a thousand grams is a kilogram (kg). So a thousand-character memory in a computer is abbreviated to, simply, K. In fact the memory is not actually a thousand at all. The

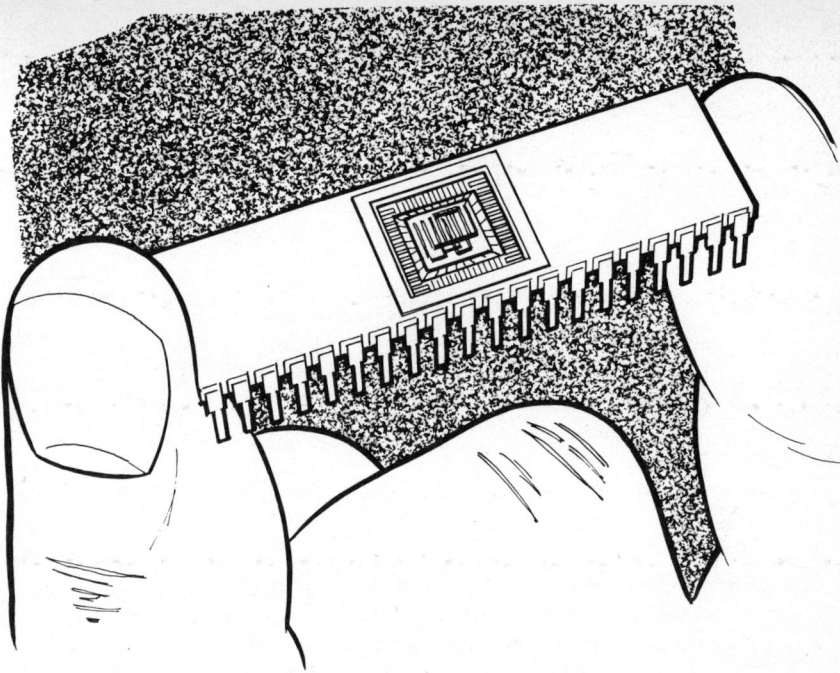

A microprocessor

computer works in multiples of 2, and if you multiply up by 2s you come to 1024 and not 1000. So a memory of 72K does not actually mean that the computer's memory can store 72000 characters, but that it can store 73728 characters. You will always get an extra 2.4 per cent to play with.

(Because of this convention, it has become smart for people to say that they earn an income of so many K. A computer programmer on £20,000 a year would say he was earning 20K, for example. In strict computer terminology, that will not do. He is actually earning a mere 19.5K (20K would be £20,480). But in the interests of fashion, who bothers about details like that?)

The computer with a 72K memory would actually be storing 72 x 1024 bytes (each eight-bit byte corresponding to a given character). So the number of separate 0 and 1 options in the memory is 72 x 1024 x 8 = 589,824 bits. Of the eight bits per byte, one is designated a parity bit and is used for checking a program. That is why the actual number of bits in an eight-bit byte is only seven, and not eight.

Bear in mind that this convention of mathematics does not tally with the modern trend towards decimalisation. Computers do not think in tens, but twos. The move towards decimalising unit systems is out of step with the future era of data handling, and if the computer's 'K' corresponds, not to 1000 but to 1024, then a new source of mathematical inaccuracy is looming up for the future, just when it is said that mathematics was one means of expressing ideas in an entirely unambiguous manner. . . .

How do I write a program?

Now at last it is time to know, to be initiated.

A program is the computer's equivalent of a knitting pattern. The pattern sets out a series of instructions which you carry out one at a time. Sometimes an established pattern is repeated; but in the end you have a garment which is the result of the carrying out of separate, step by step manouevres. A computer program has a series of instructions too, and just like the knitting pattern, where terms like 'purl' and 'plain' have a special meaning, so there are specific instructions in a computer program. Some, like RUN, are self-explanatory; RUN means 'execute the program'. Others, like RENUM , are abbreviations, in this case meaning 'renumber the program'. Some, like KILL, are jocular slang: KILL signifies 'delete a file'.

Punctuation is a crucial factor at every stage of any program. In the widely-used BASIC language, for example, if you were to instruct

PRINT "Bacon", "and eggs",

you would obtain

Bacon   and eggs

whilst if you entered, instead,

PRINT "Bacon"; "and eggs";

you would obtain

Bacon and eggs

A small alteration in setting out an instruction can make a substantial difference to the way the product appears, a point to bear in mind when you begin to use a computer for the first time.

Each stage of a program is given a number, so that it can be identified easily as the program progresses. The obvious way to do this would be to number the stages consecutively, 1, 2, 3, 4; but that is an idealistic solution. For one thing, it presupposes that the programmer is perfect. We all have second thoughts, or make mistakes; so stages in a program are numbered in larger increments, say 10, 20, 30, 40, instead. Then, if a line needs to be inserted, it can easily become 15, or whatever is appropriate to add it at the proper point.

58

A simple inter-active program can enable you to think you are conversing with the computer. It would go like this:

```
10 INPUT "What is your name";N$
20 PRINT "Hello"N$".How old are you"
30 INPUT AGE
40 PRINT "How extraordinary. You were born exactly
        AGE - 3 "years before me"
50 END
```

We once reprogrammed a set of routine instructions in a college computer so that instead of indicating, in the traditional way, something of this form:

ERROR: See page 145 of Manual

it would print

ERROR: Good grief, can't you even spell?

instead. The effect on the users was astonishing. But of course all the computer is doing is obeying instructions and printing out what it has been programmed to do. The humanoid proclivities of computers are put there by a human, and not by the machine itself, even if at times it is easy to imagine that there is a brain lurking there somewhere, watching what you are up to.

How you actually sit down to write a program is a question that can best be answered by the many manuals available. Here I am merely going to outline the idea behind it.

Your first task is to draw out an analysis of the problem. This rests on deciding what the program is going to have available, what it is going to do, and what you want to get out of it. If we take the example of the simple program we saw on p. 6, we can write down

(a) we are given two numbers, in this case 25 and 40;
(b) we are going to add those together;
(c) the idea is to find what the total is.

This could be scribbled out on a piece of paper, but with any analysis which will result in a usable program, by far the best way to start is by writing a *flowchart* which takes you through every step. There are certain outline shapes and configurations which are universally used in writing a flowchart for the solution of a problem, and it is as well to know what they are so that — in writing your own flowchart — you are following the conventions of the computer world.

In planning a simple flowchart, *operations* — which are instructions to carry out a procedure — are written in rectangular boxes, whilst *decisions*, where an option is open for consideration ('shall I, or shan't I?') are entered in upright diamond-shaped boxes. More extensive flowcharts use a fairly standard set of symbols as follows:

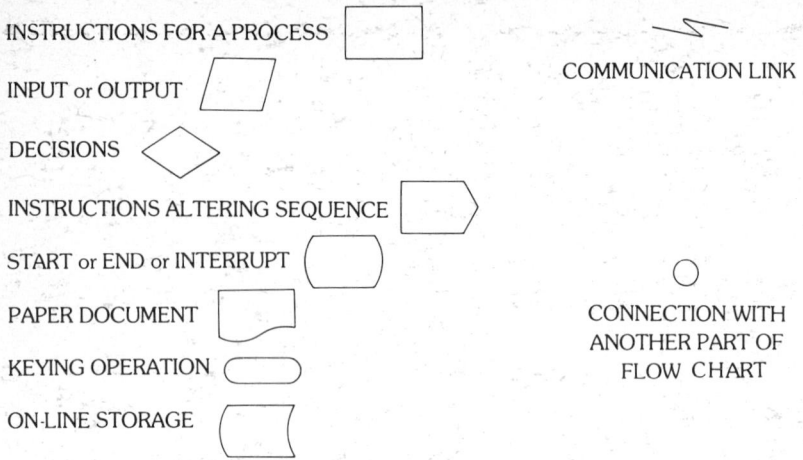

INSTRUCTIONS FOR A PROCESS

COMMUNICATION LINK

INPUT or OUTPUT

DECISIONS

INSTRUCTIONS ALTERING SEQUENCE

START or END or INTERRUPT

PAPER DOCUMENT

CONNECTION WITH
ANOTHER PART OF
FLOW CHART

KEYING OPERATION

ON-LINE STORAGE

Let us apply those now to the problem we have in hand. The flowchart would recognise that there are two INPUTS, namely the first number (25) and the second number (40). There is one INSTRUCTIONS FOR A PROCESS, which is 'add them up'; and then one OUTPUT which is the result. It would look like this:

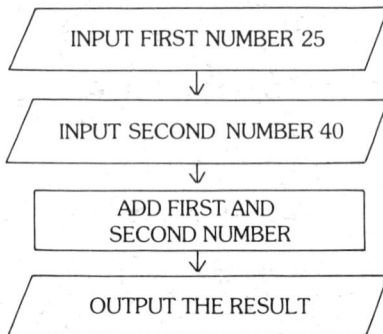

INPUT FIRST NUMBER 25

INPUT SECOND NUMBER 40

ADD FIRST AND
SECOND NUMBER

OUTPUT THE RESULT

This is the all-important first stage, and it must be completed properly.

The next task is to consider how the computer will tackle this. What instructions have we available that are appropriate to the program? What *subroutines* can be called upon (p. 71)? In what form will the output be presented?

These are easy enough to answer in the simple case of an addition program like this, of course; but as programs become increasingly complicated the planning stage can become lengthy and absorbing.

60

BUS DRIVER'S FLOWCHART

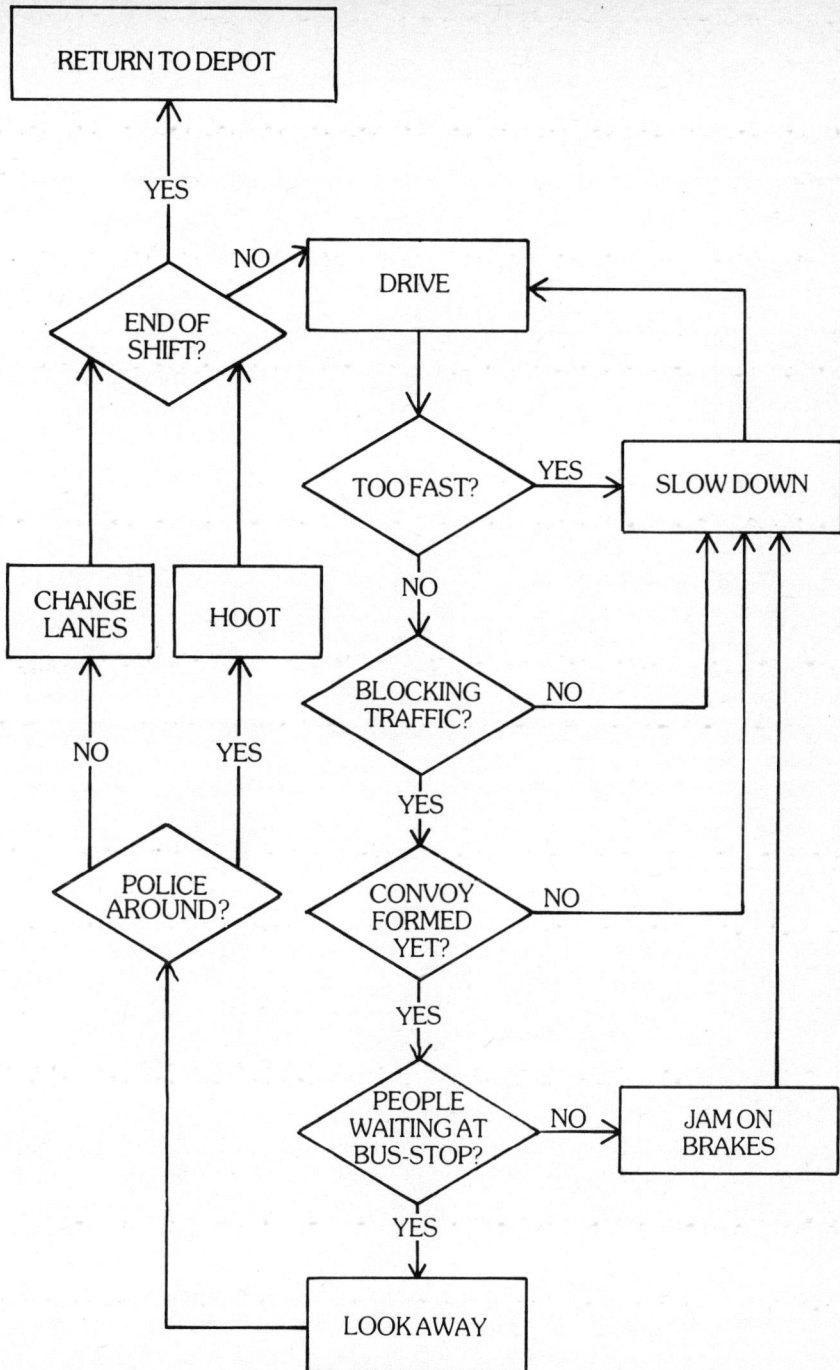

RETURN TO DEPOT

YES

END OF SHIFT?

NO → DRIVE

TOO FAST? — YES → SLOW DOWN

NO

BLOCKING TRAFFIC? — NO → SLOW DOWN

YES

CONVOY FORMED YET? — NO → SLOW DOWN

YES

PEOPLE WAITING AT BUS-STOP? — NO → JAM ON BRAKES

YES

LOOK AWAY

POLICE AROUND?

NO → CHANGE LANES

YES → HOOT

'HOW TO READ ON' FLOWCHART

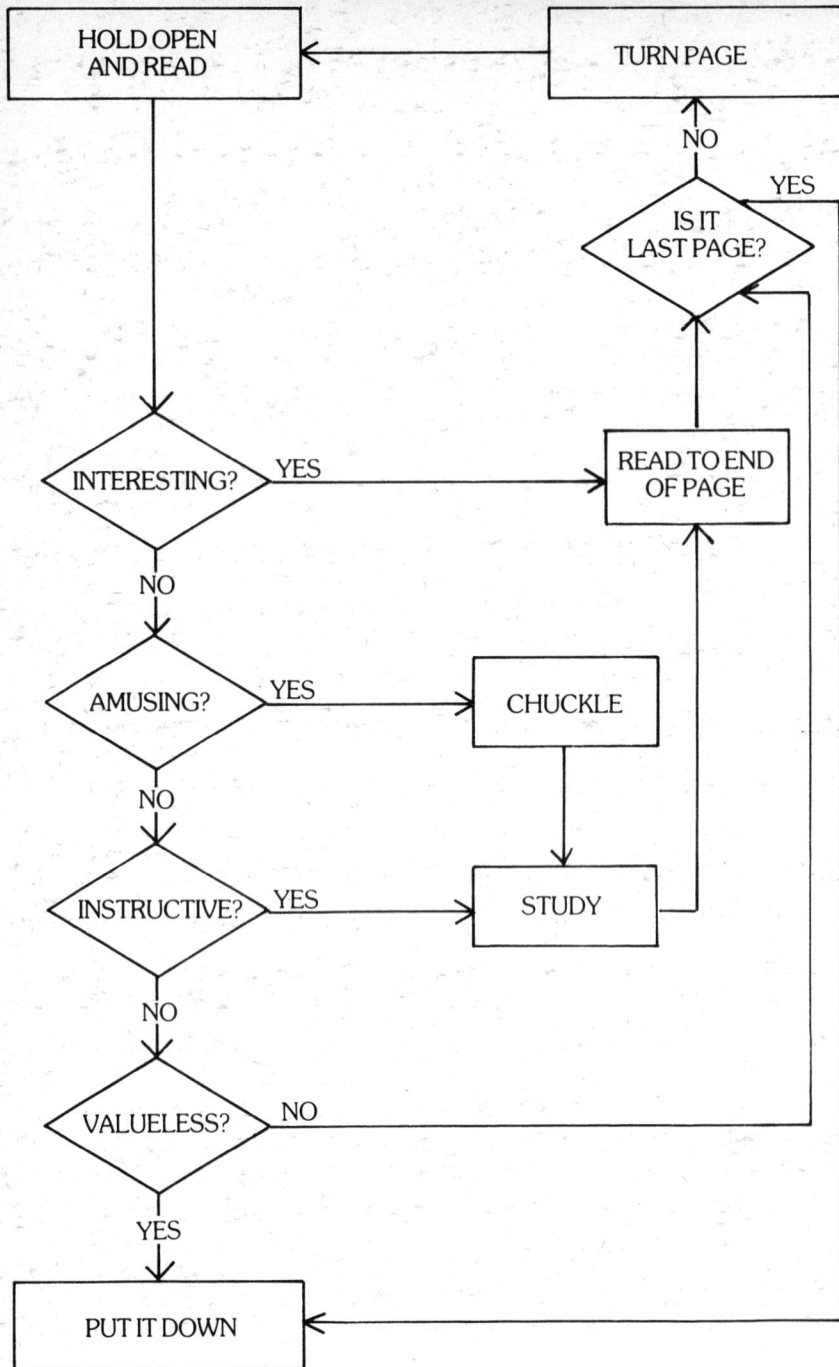

At this stage the program is actually written down. With practice, a short-hand series of mnemonics will be used which refer to procedures that the programmer understands, but does not need to write out fully. For instance, you might write RTS for 'return to subroutine', or STX meaning 'store x in memory'. The program is then written down as a machine-code list of the form appropriate to your particular computer or in a language (like BASIC) if that is appropriate, and this listing is fed into the computer.

Finally, the program is RUN .

What about bugs?

These are programming errors, and most computers are adept at spotting an inconsistency and will tell you (most politely, in some cases) what kind of mistake you have made and where you should look for an answer. A few micro-computers have been programmed so that they will not allow the programmer to continue inputting a program until the bug has been corrected. The commonest mistakes are: simple errors of punctuation which mean that letters are entered instead of numbers, or that commands are printed out rather than being acted upon; or mistakes of spelling, which has to be correct, for the computer only recognises the sequences it has been programmed to respond to, and cannot make head or tail of a word in which one letter is wrong (even though what it *ought* to say is abundantly plain to you).

The process of debugging depends on identifying exactly where in the flowchart a mistake has occurred, and for that reason the clear planning of any procedure is most important. It is deceptively simple to feel that, because you have understood a problem in your own mind, it is not worth consigning to paper. Once the flowchart is written out, and the stages you underwent in writing the program are clear, then the detection of errors that emerge later is facilitated, and debugging can become an interesting challenge rather than being a major exercise in frustration and wasted time.

What constitutes a computer language?

Computer languages express, in a form of English, specific ideas which can convey data to a computer's input. Some of the languages are designed for children (such as PILOT and LOGO). PROLOG uses a simple form of English which is close to the way people naturally speak. You can input sentences like 'Peter fights—with Jane', or 'Tim likes Tam'. COBOL (Common Business Oriented Language) was invented for commercial machines, but is being used more widely by micro users these days, whilst ALGOL (Algorithmic Language) has scientific applications. FORTRAN is a long-standing language (Formula Translator) and is a very widespread scientific language, though it does not appear in some popular modern handbooks at all. This is perhaps unfair, as it gave rise to BASIC, which is the standard micro-computer user's language of today. There are others — PASCAL, for instance — but all of them are abbreviations and conventions related to standard English. Once again, it is just like a knitting pattern: you have to learn the meanings, but once you have done so the program has its own meaning and purpose.

What is OCR?

Another abbreviation that you will hear infinitely more often than its spelt-out form: *optical character recognition.* It is the concept of knowing what a character is by looking at it, and of course that is exactly what you are doing at this very moment.

Developing a machine to perform the same task has not been easy. The first attempts were based on a specially-written alphabet with large blobs that were picked up by a scanner, and recognised as letters because of the pattern that was detected. The letters themselves were not easy to read by people, however; it took some time to get used to the typeface.

DATA-70 is a machine-readable type

(Attentive readers will recall that this was the type-face chosen by the publishers for the title of my *Cult of the Expert*, appropriately enough.)

The more up-to-date OCR-B looks more like a normal form of type, and can be read as easily by the human subject as it can be by the computer.

OCR-B is ideal

More easily, in fact; computers are traditionally better at reading marks than they are at interpreting letters and figures in conventional human-oriented form. For this reason OCR has limited applications, mostly being used on forms where it is important for the machine and the person to read the same phrase. Otherwise there is little to be saved on the normal ways of encoding data for a computer — there is little saving in keyboard time, after all, if the phrases have to be typed in. Whether they emerge as OCR letters which are read optically, or in encoded form which is accepted directly, the keyboard time is still involved. So for this reason OCR typefaces have remained of limited interest.

OMR, optical *mark* recognition, looks a more generally usable alternative. Here all the computer has to do is to recognise the position or spacing of blobs (as in the case of the earlier OCR alphabet). Here it is easy to envisage systems where students ink in a box in a multiple-choice examination paper, which can then be automatically read; or for a salesman or store-keeper to make marks on order forms to make book-keeping easier to automate. At present, OMR seems to have the makings of one of the systems we might see more of in the future.

Why do we use bar codes?

The bar code is a sophisticated form of OMR. The pattern of thick and thin lines can be picked up by an optical wand (p. 66) and converted into characters that print out to show the product reference number, the full description, and the price. In fact the price itself is not in the code, but a reference value which corresponds to the price — it is up to the retailer to program his check-out facility so that it prints the price, with the desired mark-up.

ISBN 0-241-11436-5

9 780241 114360

A typical bar code

The value of the system is clear enough to see. There is no need for the operator to enter sums into a till; all that happens is that the portion of the label with the code printed on it is passed across a little slit in the desk with a laser beneath, which reads off the code by reflecting light into the reader. The alternative long and short pattern of impulses — a kind of morse code — is then printed out for the store's use and for your reference. There can be no argument about the description of the goods, and no misplaced decimal points which can add to the bill of the unsuspecting shopper, or alternatively can make the bill unnaturally low if it is the till operator's mother or next-door neighbour who is being passed through on the cheap.

The disadvantages exist too, however, though they are not as immediately apparent. One of these is that the cost is marked on the shelf label, rather than on the goods. This makes it difficult to remember what the price of a particular brand was, if you try comparative shopping. It also makes it hard to check if the till has been incorrectly programmed, so that it is hard to challenge an incorrect listing on your bill. Labels such as '55p OFF' can be meaningless if you are none too sure whether the price indicated on the shelf refers to the new price, or the old, inclusive value. And by the time you have returned home and are faced with a large consignment of unpriced goods then, no matter how detailed and helpful-looking the bill may seem, it does not satisfy you if you simply wish to know: 'did I have my price reduction on this packet of cornflakes?'

So the laser-read bar-code tills which we were expecting to see on all sides have not yet appeared. After a rash of new supermarket developments in which the equipment was installed, British supermarkets have begun to have second thoughts and many of the most recent ones have retained the traditional till checkout. Whatever happens to the idea in the future, it is clear that customer resistance has become a force to be taken into account — and the benefits of a computer device at the drawing-board stage are not always translatable into practical reality.

How does a light pen work?

These devices look terribly sophisticated. Of course, they are; but the way they work is not at all hard to understand. The light pen is like a fat fountain-pen with a cable attached to the top end. It can be used to point at items on a television screen, and to draw lines on a designer's VDU. The ingenious part, of course, is to relate the position of the pen on the *outside* of the cathode-ray tube to the position of a signal on display on the *inside*.

At the tip of the light-pen is a transistor unit which is sensitive to light. When illuminated, it emits an electrical signal which travels down the wire. The screen itself is continuously scanned by a moving spot, producing the raster. The monitor has its own inbuilt timing system to control the raster, and the light-pen signal can be related to the timing of the raster signal. As the signal passes the region of the screen where the pen is situated, an impulse will be transmitted by the pen. That can be correlated with the position of the dot at the time, and in this way the position of the pen on the screen can be detected.

Drawing a line is not difficult, since all you have to do it ensure that the monitor generates a spot of light in the position where the light pen is detected by this timing system. In this way — as long as the pen is not moved about too rapidly, for there has to be time for the raster to transverse the screen and pick up the signal — a line can be 'drawn' across the monitor screen. In the same fashion, a given item can be 'selected' from a list of available options and keyed in to the control system of the computer itself.

The most widespread use of the light pen, however, is in the detection of bar codes. As the pen is moved across the code, the succession of bright and dark signals is transduced to a series of electrical impulses, which are read and interpreted for print-out. Within reason it does not matter how fast or slowly you move the light pen in this situation. It is even possible to scan the code the wrong way, upside-down, or at some strange angle. The impulses are instantly recognised and sorted by the computer, so you still get the correct result.

66

How do touch-sensitive video systems work?

These are excellent educational or information aids. The finest example I have seen, and one of the first to be put into operation, is the information system at the EPCOT center near Orlando, Florida (the initials stand for Experimental Prototype Community of Tomorrow, though there is not much actual 'community' about). An animated film introduces a series of boxes scattered across a screen, each containing the title of a topic in which you might be interested. Just touch the box you find interesting with your finger, and the box enlarges to fill the whole screen, and leaps into life with a video account of its own, providing further details.

What happens is that the finger's position is registered on the raster and this signal is used to trigger the replay of a film on the special topic selected. The screen of these devices is known as a 'smart screen' since it can be activated to detect the presence and position of the finger, whilst the remainder of the screen surface (the region not enclosed by the boxes shown) remains inert. Once the position of the finger has been registered, the relevant program or video recording is run and the question answered.

Ideally, a system of this sort could be used to provide an enormously complex range of information, each of the discrete segments being stored on video (if a moving film was required) or as a ROM (if a print-out of details was required). Each time you came to a multiple-choice option you could touch the screen, call up the topic of special interest, and then end up with a further multiple-choice selection. The system would be exceedingly complicated to set up, but once running it would be possible to provide rapid access to a range of visual data that is at present simply not available.

The touch-sensitive principle of the graphics tablet (p. 33) relies on a fine wire grid which is part of the screen, the position of the stylus being registered as a coordinate of the two directions in which the grid is wired. An extension of this idea would make it possible to produce a keyboard that was a touch-sensitive pad, and it is possible that some manufacturers will see this as the future for keyboard design.

Some systems already use a pressure-responsive keyboard, known as a membrane keyboard (such as the one fitted in the Sinclair ZX81), but these seem to be less satisfying to use. There is something positive about the response of a typewriter-like key, or a carefully constructed button to press. Whether that is due to our own learning process (most of us are used to typewriters before taking to computer keyboards) or whether there is actually something instinctively more acceptable about a button-operated keyboard no-one knows for sure; however it seems likely that — on present showing — the keyboard with keys will be the preferred option for a long while yet.

What are phosphors?

They are nothing directly to do with phosphorus. This element is characterised by the fact that some forms of it or its compounds glow in the dark, hence phosphorescence. Phosphors are compounds that glow when irradiated by electrons, for example, and it is this kind of material which is found on the inside of a cathode-ray screen. The cathode rays are beams of electrons, and when they strike the phosphor at the front of the tube there is an area of glowing. Enough of those produce the complete picture.

Different phosphors produce specific colours. Two popular ones for VDUs are P/31 which glows green and P/4 which is near white.

What are floppy disks?

Floppy disks are flexible plastic disks coated with magnetic recording materials. They are used like sound recordings to store data from a computer, and have the advantage of being rapid in operation: they can enter a program and store data very much faster than the cassette which is the more primitive alternative available for the micro user.

The disk was invented by scientists working at IBM, though not as part of the company's well-planned progress towards the computer age. In the words of D. A. Schon, who wrote an account of the development:

> The disk memory unit, the heart of today's random access computer, was not the logical outcome of a decision made by the IBM management. It was developed in one of our laboratories as a bootleg project — over the stern warning from management that the project had to be dropped because of budget difficulties. A handful of men ignored the warning. They broke the rules. They risked their jobs to work on a project they believed in.

The standard disk used by heavyweights in the business is not a 'floppy', but made of a metal base coated with the magnetic recording material. These are known as hard disks, and they are not usually found in personal computers. One is installed in a Tandy peripheral that can interface with their computers, and on the two 20-centimetre diameter disks (20 cm) there is a total storage capacity of over eight million bytes — 8.4 megabytes. Data can be transferred at the rate of 4,340,000 bits per second, which is enormously faster than floppy disks.

But disk systems like this are permanently installed: there is sometimes no way of removing the disks, and each has a read/write head installed either side of the disk itself.

The floppy disk is easier to use, simple to change, easy to clean and almost unbreakable. It is in essence a disk of magnetic recording tape on a plastic base. Instead of a spiralling recording track like an audio record, the tracks on a floppy disk are concentric circles which are scanned by a magnetic read/write head. As the disk spins and the head is moved across the surface at speed, it can locate and read a track within a fraction of a second, rather than requiring the time that a cassette takes to spool through the unwanted sections of a recorded program until the required zone is reached.

Each track is divided into sectors, containing 128 or 256 bytes each. The information is stored in records, which are small groups of bytes within each of the sectors. The distribution of the tracks and sectors on a disk, together with the number of bytes that can be accommodated in each sector, varies from system to system. Blank disks must be put through a process known as *formatting* by the disk operating system in each device, before the disk can be used. Pre-formatted disks are available, but they are more expensive.

The standard disk as introduced by IBM was 20 centimetres in diameter, but the disk drives to accommodate them were expensive. Most home computers now use a smaller format that is 13.7 cm across, which can store ample information. The disk drive itself is simply a box-like unit with a letter-box slot in the front. Into this goes the disk, with the label uppermost and the read/write notch towards the operator. The disk locates onto a spindle which spins it around, and the head itself travels across the surface as required. Remember that disks which have been formatted for one micro cannot, in all probability, be used in another, as there are no standards of compatibility to date. The field is further confused by the development of a new range of micro-floppy disks. IBM have one measuring 9.9 cm, and there are others measuring 9.65 cm, 8.9 cm, 8.26 cm and 7.6 cm. It is said that any of these can store more information than the home computer user's standard 13.7 cm disk. But until one of them emerges as the leader and captures the field it will be difficult to know which one to select. The incompatibility question raises its head yet again. You could invest in one system, only to find that it had become obsolete within a few years.

The question of whether you *need* a disk drive or not is related to how much use the computer has. The best way to find out is simply to use the micro of your choice with a cassette player attached to it. There is no reason to mind whilst a few moments are taken for the computer to load — but if the time does become objectionable, then the purchase of a disk drive would speed matters greatly. It is quite a good idea to dump data into a back-up — i.e., to make a duplicate copy of an important disk, just in case it is lost or accidentally erased — and a library of cassettes or disks with stored data are easily amassed.

But only time and experience will show how useful a disk drive would be to any individual.

What are buses and carts?

People keep explaining that a bus is a means of travel for computer data.

That is not where the word arose. It began life as *busbar*, a connector in an old-fashioned electrical circuit, and pronounced as 'buzz'. When multi-channel connectors were designed for computers, the same term was soon abbreviated (as is the way with jargon) and became a 'buzz' instead, soon transmuting itself to 'bus' with the soft 's'. That was because more people *read* the word first than *heard* it. It is a little like the word 'awry', which many people pronounce 'oar-y' because that is how it seems to be spelled. It is actually a wry ('a rye'). Another example is 'misled', which is a short form of miss-led, if you like; but people who have read it, rather than heard it, often say 'mizzled' instead.

In just this way the 'buzz' became a 'bus' and has been with us since.

The cart is rather different. Though it is tempting to think that this similarly means a load of fun, it is no more than an abbreviation of *cartridge*. It is in cartridge form that many programs for games are supplied. So you should certainly inquire about the range of carts available for your own prospective purchase, if playing lots of games during the long winter evenings is what you have in mind.

The range of buses is defined by the nature of the computer system. Among them are:

The Address Bus

The exact site for any set of transmitted data is known as its *address*, and an address bus is the system which directs data between the site where it is stored and the system where it is used. An address bus can have anything between four and thirty-two lines. A 4-line bus can identify 2^4 locations ($2 \times 2 \times 2 \times 2 = 16$ sites) whilst a 32-line bus copes with 2^{32} locations (i.e. 2 multiplied by itself 31 times, which is more than four thousand million).

The Data Bus

This is a collection of two-directional lines, usually four, eight or sixteen at a time. They are used to transport signals from one site to another, the exact location in each case being designated through the address bus itself.

The Control Bus

This is the centre for controlling the direction of flow of the signals between the sites in the set-up. It usually has fewer than ten lines, and can handle controlling signals of various types:

Activating signals are those which activate specific units and trigger them in sending or receiving data. An instruction in a program such as MEMORY READ is one kind of activating signal.

Clock impulses can control the timing of a sequence of operations. They may be generated by the computer, or transmitted to it from an outside source.

Interrupt signals are supplied when it is intended to halt a processing operation in full flow, in order to undertake some other task, or perhaps to add some new data. The interrupt signal might be thought of as the 'Hold the Front Page' of the computer world.

Thus the control bus is able to trigger the address bus, which then relies on the data bus system to actually take over the movement of data about.

What are sub-routines?

These are set instructions which make up a short 'program' of their own, for carrying out specific tasks. You can then key into the subroutine to bring that particular function into play, rather than having to write it out in full whenever it occurs in a program. For many purposes it is useful to have a library of them.

The subroutines you might find it useful to use include sorting instructions, to put arrays into some kind of order — alphabetical, chronological, or whatever; input, output and operating routines, to convert between decimal and binary, for controlling interrupts; or algebraic routines, covering such functions as square or cube roots, trigonometry or exponentials.

What is the difference between kW and KW?

The first of those two, kW, connotes kilowatts and is a measure of energy. A one-bar electric fire consumes one kilowatt of electricity per hour, as do ten adults in a room (though here the 1kW takes the form of metabolic energy). KW, by contrast, is a computer term connoting kilowords, or 1024 words. In most applications that the home micro user will encounter, 1KW is the same as 1KB (since most home computers have a word length of one byte). But in some computers, including a few designed for the domestic market, each word contains two bytes (16 bits), or even four bytes (32 bits). In those, therefore, there are double the bits per byte, and so the synonymity breaks down.

What is the difference between Kb and KB?

Kb means kilobits, in fact 1024 bits (p. 55). But KB refers to kilobytes. One kilobyte (actually 1024 bytes) is equivalent to about 1000 characters in your micro-computer, and is normally equivalent to 8,192 bits.

How do computers shake hands?

The term 'handshaking' is used to describe the way that two components in a system (for instance the central processing unit and a terminal) recognise each other. It takes the form of a signal sent by the receiving partner, in response to the signal which it received. In colloquial terms it is like the 'receiving you loud and clear, over!' of the movies.

When is a terminal not a terminal?

Originally a terminal was a screen and keyboard which was connected remotely to the CPU in a main computer. However, it is increasingly common to find that terminals have a limited capacity for immediate programming through the incorporation of a micro-processor. The kind that are becoming used more widely in banking and commerce are largely self-regulated, and only pass data to the main computer down the line when their own part of the business is completed.

The most primitive type of terminal is read-only or RO. It is typically a remote printer, and functions in the manner of a teleprinter. KSR terminals signify Keyboard Send-Receive, a terminal which can show data it receives, and can then transmit input through the use of a keyboard. ASR terminals are Automatic Send-Receive systems in which information can be handled on some form of internal memory device.

Are expert systems useful?

They can be useful in the right application. An expert system is one which brings together a large amount of data on a specific area of knowledge and makes it available for a specialist. They are rather like cross-referenced, up-to-date indexes. The Expert System does not involve 'intelligence' (so in that regard they are not dissimilar to the verbose and pedantic individuals I have satirised as 'experts' in another place . . .).

An expert system begins with a software facility that enables it to acquire a database, and to accept new findings as they become available; a filing structure on which the discrete items of information can fit, thus giving an inseparable relationship between the facts and their 'conceptual' framework — at least as perceived by the outsider — and a series of manipulative routines that enable the framework to be inspected, and items of data selected, that are relevant to the problem in hand. It follows, therefore, that today's expert systems are confined to the special area of interest in which each has been programmed.

Some of these systems are already in daily use, often as sources of advice on a professional level, or as diagnostic aids. There is a programme named 'Puff' which is used to assess lung function and to work out likely diagnoses in conditions of lung disease, and another which offers information on dose-rates for drugs used in heart disease.

There are expert systems which help identify distant military ships and aircraft, and this area is one which will greatly increase in the near future.

72

Others are used to advise on architectural projects, in terms of load distribution; to solve problems in pure and applied mathematics; to identify spectra; and to locate likely areas where oil deposits might be found.

It is tempting to see these as a step towards intelligent machines, but this may be an over-optimistic forecast. People often say that 'expert systems can out-perform humans in their fields' but we have to add to that an important rider — out-perform *at what?* The only facility they embody is the integration of an amount of information. They make a database accessible. There can be no doubt that they embody more actual finger-tip knowledge, of a factual kind, than a specialist in the field.

But there is little new in that. An encyclopaedia contains information that exceeds anything we might hope to carry in our own, human memories. It would be foolish to conclude from that that the *Encyclopaedia Britannica* or *Webster's Dictionary* were 'better' than a human being. They contain more knowledge, but that is why they were ever produced.

And it was mankind who recognised the need, mankind who derived the knowledge, and mankind who put it where it is. So there is little point in denigrating mankind and saying that we pale into insignificance alongside this creation of the human mind, built to store the findings of others. Henry Ford is not seen as a feeble and slow dunderhead, simply because the cars he pioneered were bigger, faster, or more long-lasting than he was. He is respected as an innovator. And I believe we should show rather less respect to the machines we have created, and a little more to the hard-working innovators who created them.

How reliable are computers?

Most people are thinking of the million-pound electricity bill sent to a pensioner with nothing but gas in the house, when they ask this question. Such faults are usually those of the operators, and not of the computers.

But there is a serious question here, for there are limits to the accuracy of any program. It is known that no series of more than 30,000 or 50,000 instructions can be guaranteed free of errors, or bugs. Many computer systems (like the Shuttle control centre, for instance) involve several million such instructions, so there can be calculated to be — literally — scores of errors lurking in the programs somewhere.

Some computer specialists I have spoken to in the States say baldly that NASA's programs are littered with bugs, some of them potentially disastrous. The answer to that from NASA is that the errors are either unimportant, or they are corrected when they do show up.

However, in spite of the fact that there are five IBM computers hooked up to the control of the Shuttle spacecraft, the list of potential problems which have reached the news media is disquieting:

1. Five days before Neil Armstrong and his crewmate took off from the lunar

surface to dock with the orbiting mother-ship, in 1969, a mistake was found in a databank. Reports said that a single character was misplaced. The effect was that the moon's gravity, which was attracting the spacecraft, would have been interpreted as a minus value instead. The effect of introducing a figure signifying that the moon was helping the module to return to earth, rather than the converse, could have been catastrophic.

2. The first shuttle flight in 1981 was postponed after a major computer failure was located. This, in front of the world's press, was a major blow and did much to undermine confidence in computers.

3. In April 1982 one of the computers on board the Challenger broke down completely. The crew were able to rely on the back-up support of the other computers aboard, but the Shuttle Commander Paul Weitz said ruefully that 'there is no such thing as a bug-free system.'

4. In December 1983, during the return flight, the Shuttle had to delay its planned landing. During the orbit, it passed directly over Siberia at a height of 80 miles. Some reporters were gleefully pointing out, after the landing, that this had been close to where the Korean Air Lines flight 007 had been shot down in September of that year. Nobody seemed to notice that the satellite was not quite at commercial airliner altitude, so the problem was not as great as all that.

But the failure of a computer system at yet another critical moment does bring home the dangers of utter reliance on electronic guidance. Your own home computer may be more modest than that, but the lesson is one worth bearing in mind.

Failure rates in new computers bought from stores for use in the home have never been fully investigated, but they seem to be unexpectedly high. A report from Business Decisions Ltd published in late 1984, for instance, claimed that a quarter of Sinclair Spectrums sold in the Boots and W H Smith stores in Britain were returned as faulty. They claimed that 18 per cent of Vic 20s and 13 per cent of Commodore 64s were returned. On this basis, it seemed that the BBC micro and the Electron were the most reliable, with a five per cent or less failure rate.

The manufacturers take a dim view of these data, as you might expect (Sinclair said that their own figures for returns were 'substantially lower' than those in the survey). But the reliability question is important and the best guide is always to have the task you wish to perform yourself demonstrated in the shop, by a specialist, on the machine you are going to buy. Not only can you then see that the application works, but that the equipment does, too.

How secure are computer systems?

Not very, would seem to be the answer. There was a time when the use of codes or passwords was guaranteed to exclude outsiders, but the clever use of computers and the experience that has been gained by enthusiasts in recent years makes them as liable to break codes as organisations are to invent them.

One classical example occurred on the evening of 2nd October 1983 during the BBCtv programme *Micro Live*. The programme was demonstrating the electronic mailbox system developed by British Telecom and known as the Telecom Gold service. It had been launched in March 1983 and by the end of the year had some 5,000 subscribers, a joint venture between Telecom and Dialcom, a United States company.

Each subscriber has a mailbox number and a password, with which to gain access to the system. The programme presenter explained on the live programme how the system was supposed to operate, emphasising its security aspect. He then approached the screen to call up the 'planted' message as a demonstration. Much to everyone's surprise, the anticipated words did not appear, for instead there was an irreverent message that had been left by a hacker who had found how to break into the circuit from his own phone at home. So much for security.

In May 1982 an American intruder faced the courts of Los Angeles, California for (among other things) an offence against Section 502 (c) of the State Penal Code involving 'computer fraud'. He was Lewis de Payne who was alleged to have penetrated the electronic security system of the US Leasing International company in San Francisco. Using his own home terminal plugged into the telephone network, he reportedly gained access to US Leasing International's time-sharing system, and then used that 'point of entry' to become a privileged user of the computer store. According to the company head, only three people — he and two others — were ever allowed to have privileged status, for it allowed them access to the details of customer's files. Mr de Payne used his entry to the system to run a program which signalled the computer to transmit to his own terminal a complete list of all the company's clients together with the passwords needed to gain access to them at any time in the future.

In what was described as his way of getting even with the company, Mr de Payne called up accounts operated by United States Instrument Rentals and destroyed some of the stores of data they contained. He then added a few obscenities and rang off, laughing. The computer was shut down for nearly two working days whilst the matter was sorted out, costing an estimated $250,000; and the programmer's time in repairing the damage and working out new security precautions added up to a further $15,000.

A third example occurred at Howardian High School in Cardiff, when the enterprising school Head, Reginald Jones, installed a computer for the training of pupils in the 1970s, long before such an idea was normal for school teaching. One of the pupils used the terminal to access the council rates office, and printed out a selection of the confidential details of rating accounts held by some of the citizens of the city, before being told to stop and go out to play rugby with the other boys.

These examples make one realise that, for all their complexity to outsiders, there is nothing about a computer data-store that is inaccessible to an enthusiast. In the past, health details and other personal matters have always been kept on file in locked filing cabinets. Obviously a friend could have access, if they worked in that office; clearly a junior clerk could catch sight of a secret memorandum. But apart from those inevitable lapses, such details were confidential and could be kept reasonably safely, away from prying eyes.

But the modern computer is likely to be connected to the phone lines for communication with input terminals and with other databases. To find out the way to break into this, a dedicated enthusiast needs nothing but his own terminal in the privacy of his home. Given time and diligence, there is almost no limit to the degree of confidentiality which could be breached by somebody determined enough.

For this reason the keeping of personal data files on computer stores should be done with discretion. It takes nothing but professional skill to write a security program, and plenty of hackers have enough ability to work out the answer to cracking it for themselves.

Meanwhile there are plans afoot to computerise a host of personal data — health records being high on the list. At the time that George Orwell wrote *1984*, he imagined that by now we would have an autocratic state which knew all about us. Though the full implications of his book have not been justified by the passage of time, that aspect certainly has. 'Big Brother' is nearer than we think.

So when new plans are mooted to transfer files to computer, I would always counsel caution. If some immense task of analysis is necessary, perhaps the concept is justified. But if not — if it is merely a question of putting the same old files into a new-looking form, for no other benefit — then we should steer away from the idea. Our privacy depends upon that. Bear that in mind if you put your own family details onto a memory which is interfaced with a telephone line!

A recent invasion of the Duke of Edinburgh's private computer-stored correspondence files, in late 1984, shows how far hackers can go in gaining entry into high-level systems through the telephone network. Currently, the Belgian government is introducing an electronic mail and information system for its Royal family, the civil service and overseas diplomatic channels to use. An advanced system of security codes will be used to prevent unauthorised access to the information. I have had 'hands-on' experience of this system, and it seems to be a fascinating new facility. But time will tell how secure it is in practice.

Can computers help in the fight against crime?

They already do. British police have access to the computer memory at

Swansea, and by calling in the registration number of a vehicle they can receive back over the radio full details of the registration details, the driver's name address age and sex, and the colour of the vehicle too. When you bear in mind the interminable length of time it takes for the same centre to process registrations and to reissue documentation, though, the use of the computer begins to look like a mixed benefit, rather than an unalloyed joy.

In Japan there has been an experiment to computerise fingerprint records. This automatic fingerprint verification computer system, AFVCS (I could imagine you working out what word those initials spelled out — sorry it is nothing pronounceable!) has already led to several important arrests. One of them was the successful indictment of an amusement-arcade attendant in Hiroshima for a murder committed more than ten years previously. In another case, an arrest was made a matter of weeks before the Japanese law on limitations would have come into force, for under their law fifteen years is the maximum length of time after the committal of an offence during which a suspect can be arrested. To date some 500 'exceptionally difficult' cases have been aided by the use of the system.

The way the system works is to measure the position of the various whorls and ridges in the print, so that these data can be stored in the computer's memory and then compared with the 800,000 fingerprints that have been taken from the police files, and fed in as the databank from which the selections are made.

There are over six million sets of prints on file in Japan, and the eventual aim is to feed all of these into the memory, adding more as time goes by. Police scientists say that they can make an identification from as little as one-tenth of the print from a single finger.

Now this is an interesting case in point. The sorting of finger-prints and the recognition of matching pairs is a tedious business, and automating the task would be a clear benefit in the solution of crime. I remain concerned, however, that so much faith is placed in such small samples of finger-print. It is true that no two finger-prints are ever alike. Neither are two snowflakes, two faces, or two flowers, when you get down to the smallest details. But the variations in a given print are not so vast that a tiny portion of a single image could not have its counterpart, especially when prints are distorted by being left on a curved object, or when the fingers have been altered by the angle of grip at the time the print was left.

The forensic science task centres on the objective analysis of data that can add weight to a case, or which, just as convincingly, can reject it out of hand. Sadly, the desire of many scientists simply to be proved right, and to succeed in carrying out whatever task they may confront as an intellectual challenge, can make the best intentioned individuals seek for links even when reasonable doubt might question them. Before such a system is adopted for world-wide use, then, let us be sure that the minimum size adopted for comparison is outside the boundaries of confusion. There is too much at stake otherwise and, as recent years have tellingly revealed, scientific evidence can secure convictions simply because it looks convincing itself.

77

By contrast, the capacity of a computer memory to store and identify data can certainly help to solve crimes involving the computer itself. One example of theft by transfer of funds to a Swiss bank account seemed, on the face of it, to be a perfect crime. A terminal operator at the London branch of a commercial bank agreed to send a command to the company's New York branch for the transfer of £5m from the London holdings to a numbered account in Geneva. The message was carefully timed to reach New York, for forwarding automatically, just before the Thanksgiving Day holiday, so that there was no time to check on the authenticity of the instruction, until three further days had elapsed. After the message had been transmitted, the operator left his work-station and travelled to the South of France to begin a luxurious holiday whilst his confederate went to the Geneva bank to collect the takings. The police were waiting, however, and both men were arrested. What they had overlooked was that the signal was stored in the originating computer in London, and it was this which bank officials decided to check during a routine inspection of the account movements. When the nature of the command was recognised, it was a simple matter to send police to intercept the collector in Geneva, for the bank account number which he had used was stored too and gave an unarguable identification. As a plot for a film, the plan would have worked admirably. In the real world, however, it was no match for the computer's simple, but reliable, memory. The domestic micro can record transactions just as indelibly, of course.

Can computers aid criminals?

That question is easier to answer. Within a decade or two, I believe almost every fraud will involve a computer somewhere, because so many of them will be in use and there will be no end to the opportunities for illicit entry into data banks amongst those who are clever enough to think a way round the problem. The principles on which computer crime is based seem to be many. But some points to remember, if you think you stand a chance of becoming a victim yourself, are these:

a) Remember that programs, both your own, and those written by or used by criminals, can be made to self-destruct. Some commercial systems, for instance, are programmed to wipe themselves out if a rental or renewal fee is not paid on time. Other programs have been written that carry out a crime, and then instruct the memory to erase the fact that they ever existed. (A version of this could perhaps have made an important difference to the outcome of the crime I described above.) Alternatively, an outsider could gain access to a program and key in a destruction code which caused damage to your own procedures, even if nothing else was done. Whether your intention is to use a micro at home or at work, the destruction of programs is a vital element of security.

b) Bear in mind that 'little and often' techniques are hard to detect. Rather than milk an account of a single large sum, for instance, a programmer might decide to reduce many sums of money by a small, scarcely noticeable, amount. Suppose you were to trim off 2 per cent of all conversion factors applied to commercial, international trading for instance. The fact that the converted sums were somewhat lower than had been expected would probably be missed altogether. If not, it would be ascribed to a dip in the exchange rate.

But the small sums that were left would accumulate to produce a large total, and there could be no way in which the authorship of the event might be identified if the program was destroyed after the manoeuvres themselves were over. One such crime has already been recorded. It was carried out by a rates clerk, who realised that the rounding-up and rounding-down of figures in the accounts left the small extra sums looking for a home. He programmed the computer to accumulate these in each successive entry, inserting a mythical code name which began with two Zz's of his own at the end. In this way all the odd, left-over sums accumulated, and he put one stage in the program that caused it to self-destruct if it was run by anyone.

Hackers call this the 'salami method': it rests on small, thin slices of action spread over a number of targets. Their expression, 'piggy-backing', refers to the technique of finding a password or an entry code and using that to gain access to programmes or stored data files.

One specialist confidently told me that undetected computer crime in Britain costs around a million pounds per year. I responded by pointing out that if the crimes were 'undetected' it did not say much for the accuracy of his figures — but it is still an indication of the problem.

The only reliable data that seems to be available is figures from a survey carried out by the Local Government Audit Inspectorate which was published in 1981. They asked over 300 organisations to account for the losses they had sustained through computer fraud. Twenty per cent replied, saying that their own data banks had been interfered with. The total losses over a five-year period had been in excess of £1m. A report on computer crime in the United States and dating from the mid 1970s calculated that as much as £30m was being lost each year throughout Europe and the United States combined, and the present rate of reported losses throughout American computer crime is as much as $100m a year.

How much in addition to that goes undetected? As I said earlier, nobody can ever know. But it could easily be eight times as great, so the US total would amount to $800m. Now, the highest estimate I have seen was $3,000m per year, and that may well be over the top. But in either cases the losses are substantial.

There is a level of pride which deters people from reporting crime carried out against them by somebody who has literally outwitted their own procedures. Ask yourself: would you be keen to admit to a policeman that you had been out-smarted by some other enthusiast? Where computers are a matter of personal pride and prestige, which is often the case, people tend to keep quiet about such matters.

Another psychological problem is that losses are anticipated, almost expected, of a successful enterprise, large or small. Shop owners speak of shop-lifting euphemistically as 'shrinkage', and four or five per cent is regarded as the going rate for a retail business. I have been told that a level of petty theft like this is regarded as the sign that a business is flourishing. Unless there are crowds, shop-lifters do not come into a store. And unless the presentation and display of the goods is inviting, people do not pilfer. Too low a figure, which you might think was every shop-keeper's aim, could be taken as a slight either on the success of his establishment in pulling the crowds, or a condemnation of his ability to display goods invitingly.

Once this kind of mentality is prevalent, then the loss of resources through a 'tolerable' level of computer fraud is not immediately guarded against. And of course, there is a tendency to 'admire' anyone who 'beats the system'. There is one story (which I am told is not merely an apocryphal tale) that students in a computer course were encouraged to break into data banks and extract information from them as part of their training. One of the students gained access to the college's own progress files, and entered a 100% mark and distinction against his own name. Needless to say, he was regarded as a star pupil and soon found himself a senior post in a giant manufacturing organisation. There is a strange moral code at work there: how many pupils, after showing how they had secretly entered with headmaster's rooms, would be given job security and a pension as a reward?

A serious potential threat comes from something called block mode transmission. This is a form of instruction in which a whole block of data can be transmitted to the source of a signal, recognised by the computer as 'host'. Hackers can gain access to the circuitry through a telephone input, and then simply dodge around until the right technique emerges. From then on the data would be transferred to the 'parasite', and he could then use the data bank as though he were actually the rightful owner. In many cases (since he could presumably channel requests for link-ups through to his own terminal) the system could continue running without anyone knowing what had happened. And whilst the unauthorised user was in command, he would be the *de facto* 'owner' of the data.

It seems perfectly feasible that an amateur using a few disk drives with plenty of storage capacity could obtain access to an on-line computer, transfer all the input and output to his own terminal, and use it for as long as he wished. He could then destroy the original, keep his own 'copy', and it would be exceedingly difficult to tell *either* that he had done such a thing, *or*, even if you did, that he was not the rightful owner. Copyright in such things has yet to be legally recognised.

Part of the problem is that the people who are frequently concerned with these procedures are not those who program the machines. The individual

80

whose responsibility it is to ensure that records are kept confidential, for instance, is a manager. How many managers are conversant with what computers can do? The managerial responsibility will have to widen in the years ahead, and so familiarity through the use of a micro at home is one way to anticipate that change.

In the same way, how many accountants are used to understanding what goes on in a computer system? Accountants are concerned with paper, with facts and figures, and not so much with computer programming. The closest inspection of the paperwork on what goes into a computer, and what comes out, may bear little resemblance to what is happening whilst the computer is running — if there is a rogue, acquisitive personal routine in the program that is lining someone's pocket, for instance.

And if the accountant does want to look closer, he cannot do so unaided. He relies on the programmer or the technician to operate the inputs and outputs, which prevents the accountant himself from prying too closely into what is going on. In no other field would any financial analyst be allowed to remain remote from the essential data under consideration.

Many crimes have been based on the shortcomings of the paperwork that computers generate. The automatic codes on cheques and paying-in slips provide cases in point. Frauds using cheques have been carried out by clerks who worked in the section of a bank responsible for the processing of cheques with defaced machine-readable codes. There is always a proportion of these in any day's work.

The plan was that the clerks would go to distant branches of the banks and obtain cash withdrawals, after starting up their own bank accounts in the branch concerned. They would subtly deface the code on each cheque. Eventually, the cheque would fail to be machine-read, and so would be passed to them for manual clearance. All they had to do was lose the cheque in a pocket and dispose of it later. All record of the transaction ended at that moment, and so their accounts were never debited with the sum they had withdrawn.

Paying-in slips were used in a number of American bank frauds. The technique was simple: a bank customer would go round a few banks in his area and leave one or two of his own paying-in slips at the bank counter, along with those already put out for the benefit of customers without a paying-in book to hand. The customer would fill in the details of the account, enter the sum, the name and address . . . and would then pay in money in the normal way.

But of course, the codes on the slip were machine-read. As a result, the sums were diverted to the wrong account (the 'right' account, if you are on the side of the perpetrator of the act) in spite of what was written on the slip.

It is worth noting, incidentally, that you can now buy insurance against losses through somebody getting access to your computer. However, if the trends continue it may be that the premiums will increase over the next few years.

It is not just through electronics that fraud is perpetrated in the computer world. Bribes have been offered to bank employees by criminals who wanted a list of account codes, so that they could gain access to funds belonging to someone else. There have been cases of lists of key words, passwords and security codes being stuck to the side of a console, where it was handy for the operator, but also where the vital clues were available for intruders (or cleaners) to copy down. In one example a snapshot was taken — but with a high-definition Olympus camera — and from an enlargement all the security data was read off.

Floppy disks are easy to conceal, and in some cases they have been stolen. Since one disk looks much like another, it is possible to exchange any disk for a similar-looking one. (It would be just as easy to exchange one disk for another bearing some embarrassing program in place of the one which was supposed to be present, though I have never heard of that being done to date).

And then there is always the ultimate — stealing the whole computer! Micros are much in demand these days, and the theft of a computer from your home is a real possibility. Though you might be insured against the loss of the machine itself, there is no cover for the amount of time you might spend in recovering missing data files. Meanwhile it is true that, just as miniaturisation has made computers cheaper to buy, less expensive to run, and smaller and more compact, it has also made them much easier to steal.

But so much information is now being stored in giant data banks, with possible access through telephone networks, that I have no doubt that within a few years there will be a flood of new-wave crimes involving computer fraud. If you are involved with setting up a new system at the office, bear this in mind. Tomorrow's computer frauds will make yesterday's great robberies look like short-changing the collection plate. I would bet on it (in cash, of course).

So my micro can speak to other computers. Will it ever speak to me?

It might well, and sooner than you think. Synthesised voices have been available for a decade or more, and one familiar type of product using the principle are the computerised tutors that teach youngsters how to master spelling or mathematics by calling out the problem, and then going through it until the right answer emerges (either given by the child, or revealed by the machine itself). Other versions have been installed in high-tech motor-cars, with steely detached voices that remind you to 'fasten seat belt' or 'close rear door'.

Modules that can interface with computers are beginning to reach the shops. Within the device is a sound-generator whose output is modified through a dynamic filter, producing the synthetic speech. Words typed in by the operator will be read out by the voice. This is ideal for the visually handicapped, useful for issuing warnings to staff who may not be watching a screen for instructions, and a wonderful way to impress friends who are just as crazy for the latest computer gadgetry, but have yet to obtain one themselves. A built-in polyphonic sound generator is featured in the Macintosh computer, for instance, which enterprising hackers will find appealing.

The future for speech synthesisers may be very rosy. The type of unit installed in children's toys which teach spelling and simple mathematics are only a start. They function by producing the essential components of speech, known as allophones, from ROM components in which they are stored. The result is a tinny voice that sounds like something from a bad space film, rather than a sympathetic partner in education.

Speech is produced by more subtle means than this, via nose and larynx, the echoes of sinuses, the shaping of the palate, as well as just the lips, tongue and vocal chords, and current research, mostly in Japan, is investigating the ways in which we might more closely approach this natural speech-production. The idea is to generate a vocal-chord wave-form in an acoustic chamber which simulates the contours of the human voice tract. In this system, a series of baffles would modulate the sound, and then — controlled by computer — would help produce a voice that was more natural.

Until then, we are left with speech synthesisers like the module produced by General Instruments, containing a 16K ROM of sixty-four allophones, a modulator to generate digital sound output and a control system to integrate the results into words. It is not much, compared with what we have yet to experience. It is, though, a start.

5 Kids' Stuff — Computers and Education

Are computers useful for education at home?

In an era when computers are everywhere in schools (95 per cent of British schools had one in 1984, for example) there is a clear repercussion at home. Should parents buy one for the child to use at home? Or, since there *is* a computer at school, would that be a sheer waste of time (and money)?

On the positive side, there is certainly no damage to a child who lacks a computer at home. Many young parents like to feel they are in contact with the latest trends, and I have sometimes wondered whether the latest computer — together with state-of-the-art peripherals — is replacing the latest car as the domestic status symbol of tomorrow. Like electric railway sets once, there is the possibility that father buys the latest computer to play with himself, whilst pretending it is for the kids. There are many schoolchildren who find they cannot get near the machine as long as there is a challenge to be overcome — father is at work in the spare room, building programs of awesome complexity, or typing on a word-processing system letters and memoranda that used to take a few seconds, and now seem to take hours instead.

The problem with the school micro is that much the same has happened there: the device has been bought by the trendy teacher, and it is the teacher who uses it most. Take a class of twenty-five, with four lessons per week of 40 minutes each during which computer training is given, and that will amount to $4 \times 40 \div 25 = 6.4$ minutes 'hands-on' experience each, on average. Take out the time that the teacher would use in explaining procedure, and you might have less than three minutes a week for each child actually using the computer. In that situation, a home-based device would be the only way that the pupil could have a reasonable amount of time to herself.

Many schools now use Tandy or BBC micros, and it would obviously be helpful to choose a model that was the same as the one used in school, if you wished to give your child the chance to use one at home. There are smaller and cheaper computers on sale, like the little Sinclair ZX type; but it might be inadvisable to buy a device which was much more limited in scope than the one at school, for the simple reason that the child might be unable to practice much of what had been learned during the day.

84

There are some new computer languages, like PILOT and LOGO, which have been developed for use in schools. The everyday language of the home computer is BASIC, however, and it would clearly be helpful to know that the model you were thinking of buying was compatible with what the children were being taught at school. There is much to be said for using computers, in the sense that they prepare children for a career in that burgeoning field; but the actual validity of the computer in the educational process itself is harder to justify.

There are many people who insist that the computer excels as a pure teaching aid, but this I doubt. Programmed learning came in over twenty years ago, when a student would grasp a passage of instruction and then have to satisfy a series of separate questions before going on to the next stage. But these programs were published in book form, so that the student could use the aid as a textbook, on a train or at the desk. Transferring all that to a computer is a laborious and expensive way of doing much the same thing and there is little to convince me it does the job that much better.

The one redeeming feature that might enter into the argument is that children caught up in the craze might well be more motivated to learn. In that sense a slow reader, a poor speller or a backward mathematics student could well improve special skills by using an educational program in this way. It would not be that the form of teaching was any better than before, just that — being a computer! — it might be construed by the child as being more fun. That, in the end, is the key to all successful teaching.

Why are children so good with computers?

Two reasons. One is that they start using them in schools, when the mind is untrammelled and the brain's own thinking mechanisms are ready for instruction of that kind. Adults often find their thinking processes are limited by habit of a different kind, and children can pick things up more quickly if the mind is receptive, and untroubled by preoccupations. Look how fast a child learns a language, for example.

The other reason is *not* because the children who are so clever using computers are some kind of genius. The child mind works in a systematic, step-by-step way, whereas an adult is better at what I call 'total vision' — the holding of a complex mass of interrelated data as a mental 'pattern'. Computers work step by step, in a methodical way, which in some ways is closer to the mind of a child. So the reason why youngsters are proficient at using computers is not because their minds are somehow super-intelligent at all; it is because they are receptive, and because computers and their programs work in the essentially simple fashion, one step at a time.

There are innumerable tales of schoolchildren who have made a fortune out of computer games. One such game, Orbiter, was invented by 16-year-old Andrew Glaister of Crawley, West Sussex. Whilst at school he estimated he was earning at the rate of more than £50,000 per year, largely from a twenty-five per cent royalty paid on the sale of each of the games. Patience, flair and method are the answer.

Why are there so many more males in computers than females?

The obvious reason is that teachers have traditionally associated specific subjects as being of 'natural' interest to boys and not to girls — and vice-versa, of course. That would explain much of the trend to funnel the genders into their own categories of education.

However that is not, in my view, the whole answer here. You have also to look at the characteristics of the field. To be a computer freak, a true 'hacker', you need qualities of obsessiveness. My own research into sexual preferences tends to confirm that boys are biologically more likely to be obsessive than girls. That does not mean that all boys are like it, or that no girl can be obsessive too; what I speak of here is a trend within the two sexes and nothing more. So that is one reason why females *on average* might be less likely to lean towards the computer as a focus of obsessive interest.

The second factor which comes into play is the essentially materialistic appeal of computers. To acquire one can be a response to an instinctive desire to keep up with the possessions of a friend, and many of the peripherals are acquired as much for their attractiveness as possessions, as for their value in practice. That argument applies to the ownership of the micro too, clearly. Many of the uses to which micros are put in the home are comic exaggerations of the best and quickest way to do a job. As an example, the translation programs people carry around with them, or the word files some use, are feeble alongside even an ordinary pocket dictionary. The time it takes to activate a computer, enter the relevant software, type in the desired word and obtain the translation is much more than the act of removing a dictionary from your pocket and flicking to the right page.

Once a computer is owned, it inevitably collects accessories of one kind or another to gratify the owner. This characteristic, I believe, is more likely to occur in males than in females, simply because males are apparently more materialistic.

Those two factors — obsessiveness and acquisitiveness — might account for a bias towards males in the computer world. If so, then for all the much-needed reform of our educational system, we are always going to find more men interested in the field than women. You could say that this was because females often find the whole thing beneath them, or that they are (to adopt a biased attitude) too bright to bother with something so mundane. Now I am not going to argue with that.

What examinations should my children pass to become programmers?

The first question here is whether they actually *want* to become programmers. It must be a tremendously stimulating job for someone cut out for it, but it would have the makings of a slow and painful retirement from reality if it was forced upon somebody by misguided parents. There is a lot of this about.

Many of the childhood prodigy programmers, who have made their fortunes out of video games, showed their promise at home, or in school, and simply sold their products when they had already produced them. This is a great liberating fact about the home computer: it puts computing power into the hands of everyone, and there is no need to worry unduly about academic attainments if a child is in that category.

The essential 'O'-levels that should be aimed for are Mathematics, Physics and English Language. Passes at CSE are often acceptable. But (and this is the point) a top-rank programmer does not need to fall back on such attestations of prowess, for he or she simply *does* it. It is a little like asking what GCEs you would need to become a concert pianist, or which CSE certificates help to establish one as a world-class ice-skater. Those with extra abilities simply demonstrate the fact. In the computer field, Sir Clive Sinclair never even went to a university.

Are computers going to make children illiterate?

Many people fear that the answer is 'yes'. Much has been said of the paperless office, and of screens where words and concepts magically appear so that nobody has to write, spell, or to actually *do* anything any more. That seems a frightening prospect to many, particularly older, people. The reality is very different.

Of course there can be no argument that children of the near future can abandon literacy, if their computers will do it all for them. No child can generate input without being able to spell, for a misspelt word would be rejected by a computer. A child needs to be able to type, too; and so an art long associated with dim-witted girls has suddenly become the hallmark of the bright, sparkling tycoon of today. How peculiar it is that our prejudice can switch around so dramatically.

The use of a computer terminal will necessitate a reasonable level of literacy, therefore, rather than removing it altogether. And for literate, numerate people (which includes almost everyone who has access to this book), the computer era should hold no terrors. The claim has been made that the illiterate were left out when printing was invented; and now the computer-blind will be similarly left out of tomorrow. That is nonsense. Computers generate information which anybody can read. If the message is not clear, then that is the fault of the programmer who produced the print-out in muddled form. There is no comparison to be made between an illiterate person and a book, or a non-computer trained individual and a terminal. If you can read normally, then you have access to both.

The only problem — and it is a small one, easily overcome — is to become familiar with the way the terminals operate. I say this in a cautionary way because of a friend who was one of the first to possess a cash card for a bank dispenser terminal. When he approached it and read 'INSERT CARD' he did so. Several times. Eventually he managed to do it the right way round. It then said 'KEY IN YOUR IDENTIFICATION NUMBER', which he managed well enough. But then came the difficult part. 'INDICATE SUM REQUIRED IN MULTIPLES OF £5,' said the screen. He wanted £15, and so he pressed the £5 key (as he thought) three times. Up came the sum, '£555'. In his haste, he says, he pressed the 'ENTER' key and the way he tells the tale the machine ran out of five-pound notes long before it had got half-way through his order. I have never come across a machine like that subsequently, I admit; but it is a nice story.

'User-friendly' is the term applied to the current move to make computers less intimidating to the novice. They can be irritatingly over-familiar (some computer programs have phrases like 'ENJOY YOURSELF' or 'HAVE A NICE DAY' liberally sprinkled into the printout at strategic points), but it is certainly better to read 'YOU NEED A NUMBER AT THIS POINT: TRY AGAIN' rather than 'ERROR 999 BAD INPUT'.

What are those strange words computer fans use?

Computers have spawned their own culture. The mentality of the programmer, the obsessiveness of the hacker have all given rise to in-talk, to buzz words of the most esoteric kind. And why not? Most groups with special interests have done precisely the same in the past, and computer enthusiasts need be no exception.

Some of the words are easy enough to interpret, like 'spazz', which can be a noun or a verb. It means 'to behave oddly' and arose from the word spastic — tactlessly, you might think. 'Crufty' means tacky, badly built; a 'frobnitz' (plural: 'frobnitzem', rather strangely) is a small physical object (we always call them 'glodgetts' in our family); 'crashing' is when things go wrong; whilst to complain is to 'gritch'.

A 'gating event' is a crucial moment, whilst to 'interface' means to meet and discuss something. 'Windowing' is the technique of keeping several balls in the air at once — professionally speaking, that is — whilst to 'core dump' means letting go and speaking frankly about what has been bothering you. The term 'bandwidth' is used to connote someone's mental ability — 'narrow bandwidth' means stupid, whilst 'broad' or 'big bandwidth' means intelligent.

Computer people are often short on literacy. Thus discs are spelt disks these days, and nouns often become verbs whilst nobody is watching. Thus an interface is a zone of contact. But in computerese there is a verb 'to interface' (see above). A key factor can be described as being 'really very key'.

88

Garbage collector, abbreviated to 'GC', has long been used for the disposal of unwanted material, and that too finds a quasi-verbal place in the dictionary. 'I am going to GC the office' means that it is going to be spring-cleaned.

There is nothing new in this, though. Was it not Patrick Campbell who wrote explaining how 'a goss on the potted meat' was a perfectly understandable term to devotees of croquet? It was, he patiently explained, a way of describing a soft stroke — like gossamer, hence 'goss' — on a ball that was a brownish colour (like potted meat). So, in the middle of a game, the cautionary advice 'try a goss on the potted meat' made perfect sense. So do most of these other terms. They are fun, that's all.

Some terms now have a dated sound. They include electronic, on-line, assembler, even data-bank; but terms like network, user-friendly, bit-twiddle, and ergonomic are becoming very fashionable. Computer freaks keep up with all this, of course. Their credibility depends on it.

6 Serious Stuff — Some Technical Ideas

What is a diode, and where do diodes belong in computers?

The original form of a diode was a glass wireless valve similar in some ways to a light-bulb. But it was a light-bulb with a difference: instead of merely having a filament which glows when a current passes through it, the valve was fitted with a collector plate for electrons.

A hot wire (like the filament of a lamp) gives off electrons. If there is a collector near the filament, with a positive electrical charge which will attract the electrons, then a current can flow as electrons leave the glowing filament, or emitter, and are picked up by the plate, or collector. An electric current is made up of moving electrons, and so a continuous flow from the emitter to the collector can occur.

But now, suppose instead that the plate is made negative in charge. Electrons carry a negative charge, and so they will be repelled by the plate. The plate itself does not heat up to become an emitter, so no electrons are going to escape from it; and even if they did, they would not be attracted to the filament, for that is already trying to get rid of electrons as far as it can. In this alternative condition, then, no current can flow.

We have here the basis of a valve, that is, a system which allows current to flow one way, but not the other. A bicycle tyre valve is a more familiar example: pressure from outside can force air in, but pressure from inside cannot force air out. The flow is one way only: and that is the definition of a valve. Alternating electric currents are familiar to us, mainly because the mains itself is in the form of alternating current. The electrical current flows one way, then drops to zero, and then flows in the opposite direction. It changes in this way fifty times per second (which gives rise to that low hum, the 'AC hum' or 'mains hum' that you can often hear in electrical devices). But if a valve was put into the circuit, then the current would be able to flow in one direction only. The alternating current has been, as we say, *rectified*. And it was as a rectifier that these valves were used.

Clearly, since each of these valves had two electrodes, it was obvious that they would be called *diodes*. Their uses were many, but such diodes are made of glass, they contain wires; they can burn out, get broken, leak or fade

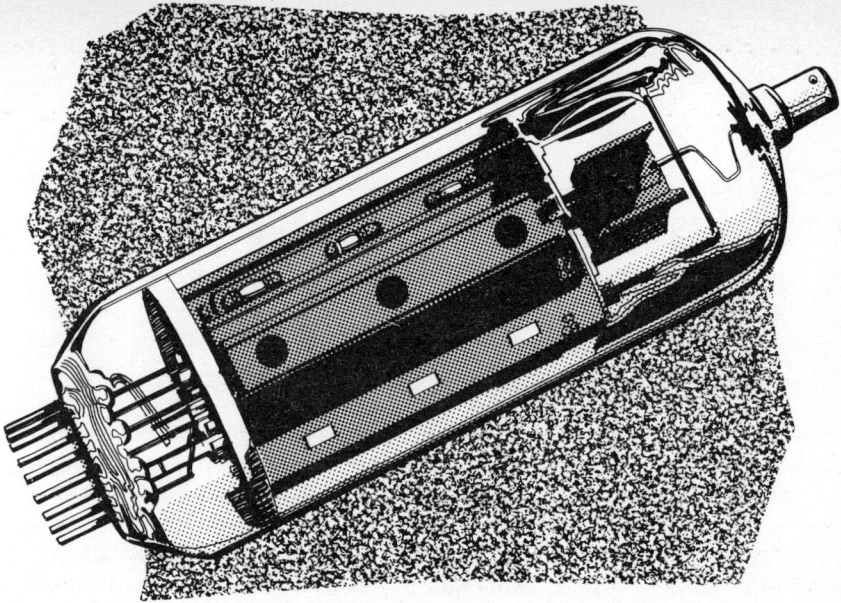

A wireless valve diode

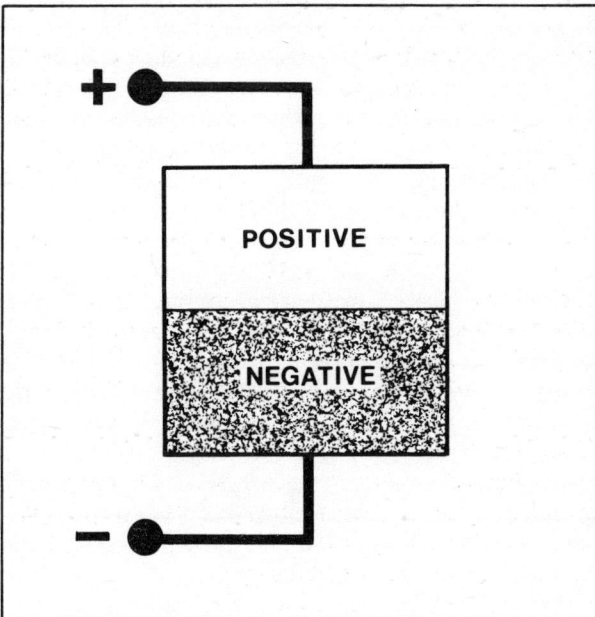

A silicon diode

with use. What was needed was a solid and virtually unbreakable form of diode. And this came about through the development of *solid-state physics*.

It was found that it was possible to 'dope' the element of silicon with traces of impurities. Using elements such as phosphorus or antimony, the effect of a slight contamination of pure silicon is that the silicon possesses an awkward number of extra electrons. Conversely, if a different 'impurity' is chosen (such as indium or boron) the silicon that results would have an electron deficiency. It is easier to think of these deficiencies as 'holes', waiting for an electron to come along and restore the *status quo*.

Doped silicon is a reasonably good conductor of electricity, because these extra electrons and holes are easily set into motion. In fact, pure silicon, without being 'doped', is a poor conductor of electricity because it holds on to its electrons. Now let us see what happens when we sandwich some positively doped silicon (with 'holes') to some that is negatively doped (with extra electrons), and try to pass a current across the face between them.

If the current flows one way, we will have no problem. The negative charge will pass into the negatively doped side of the diode, driving the electrons across the great divide and into the holes that are awaiting them. In this way the circuit is established, and the current will flow as though the diode is a switch in the 'on' position. But when the current reverses its direction, the flow of current is terminated.

The effect then is that the positive charge applied to the negatively-doped silicon will at once attract electrons. Like charges repel, remember, and unlike charges attract. At the same time, the negative side of the diode has now a positive charge applied, and that will attract the holes. In this way the electrons and the sites where they would be received are attracted *away* from each other. In this condition, the interface is left denuded of participants to the reaction we encountered before, and so no current can flow.

In this way we have made a solid-state diode which can be dropped, bitten, sat on, thrown, or treated badly in any one of a hundred other ways. It will not leak, or break open, because it is made of solid pieces of silicon compound. So here we have a valve which can be made much smaller, much more cheaply, and more quickly than the old-fashioned glass version; and which will perform more predictably too.

Some materials can be used in diodes which glow when the electrons recombine with the sites where they belong. In these materials (such as gallium arsenide, which is a popular example) the electrons enter a conducting mode when they are passing an electrical current, but return to a valency band, as it is called, when they recombine with the atoms where they belong. This shift releases energy in the form of light, and the compound glows. This principle has been harnessed to provide illuminated read-out components in a range of devices, clock-radios being a familiar application. These were originally used for the dials of digital watches, now superseded by liquid crystal displays. But that is what a light-emitting diode (LED) really is; and I hope it seems less intimidating and mysterious now than it did before.

LED technology still has a wide range of actual and possible applications however, one of which has frequently been discussed. This is the idea of the flat-screen television. When this was first suggested, it was clear that a bundle of LED units collected together could be made to glow in response to an applied current and in this way build up a coherent television picture. But there is a similar process which has greater promise.

This is the gas plasma screen. It works on the same principle as a fluorescent tube. The screen is made of a sandwich of a fluorescent material like zinc suplhite, between two conducting layers, one opaque and the other transparent. When a current flows between adjacent points on the conductors, passing through the zinc sulphite layer, then a glowing spot will appear. This is an example of fluorescence, however, and not of the radiant recombination effect which we encountered in the LED.

The possibility certainly exists here to manufacture a thin, flat TV screen that would be less costly to manufacture and much less vulnerable than a conventional cathode-ray tube. The most popular of the miniature flat-screen televisions of the present day has been designed by Sinclair Electronics of Cambridge. The complete device is the size of a transistor radio. Here, though, a normal cathode-ray principle is utilised. The tube has the screen twisted sideways, so that the whole unit is flatter than the 'ice-cream cone' shape with which we are familiar, and the signal is spread out in a wedge-shape to counteract the distortion on the screen which would otherwise result. The picture is viewed from the back of the screen through a lens which magnifies it. Although this is certainly a small television set, then, it does not represent any technological breakthrough in principle. Of the many alternatives available in theory, including versions of the liquid-crystal principle, I think I would put my money on the gas plasma screen. With the right choice of fluorescent materials a colour screen that was flat and thin would be perfectly feasible.

Where do relays fit in?

Relays were the first kind of electrical substitute for the mechanical gears and cylinders of the mechanical calculating devices of the eighteenth and nineteenth centuries. A relay is a switch, and the principle has many applications in the world of technology.

The simplest version is a coil of copper wound around a soft iron rod for its core. If a current flows through the coil, then the iron will become magnetised, but if the current stops then the magnetic effect vanishes and the iron returns to its at-rest, inert, non-magnetised state. Near one end of the core is a switch, normally held in the open or 'off' position by a spring. When the core of the relay is magnetised, the arm of the switch is drawn across and the switch itself closes. In this way, a current can now flow across the circuit. But if the coil is switched off again, the core loses its magnetic attraction for the switch unit, which immediately springs open again, cutting off the current it carried.

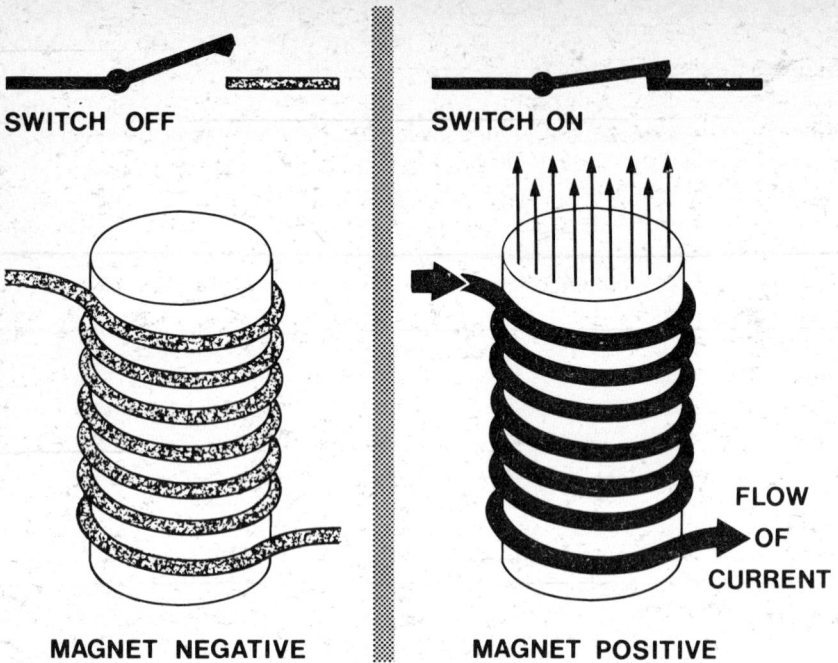

SWITCH OFF   SWITCH ON

MAGNET NEGATIVE   MAGNET POSITIVE

FLOW
OF
CURRENT

How a relay works

The most familiar example of this idea is an electric buzzer or doorbell (not the kind that merely go 'ding dong', the kind with a continuous whirring ring). This works simply by having the current in the main coil switched on and off by the switch alongside, and that in turn is fitted with a striker for the bell. As soon as the current flows — when the bell-push is pressed — the iron core becomes magnetised, the switch unit is attracted, and as that happens the striker hits the bell. But at this moment, the movement of the switch unit cuts off the current flow, so switching off the coil, cutting the magnetic pull, and allowing the arm to fall back to the resting position. As soon as that happens the current flow is re-established, the coil is energised once more, and the whole cycle repeats itself. In this way the bell sounds for as long as the current is supplied by the pressing of the bell-push.

The electric 'ding dong' bell works in a related fashion. In this case, as the bell is rung and the current flows, the coil becomes magnetised and forces the core — in this case moveable — to strike one of the sounding bars of the bell. The device is designed so that the striker hits it once only, and then falls back a little way, allowing the 'bell' to sound clearly. When the pressure is removed from the bell-push and the current is interrupted, the striker falls back, propelled by a spring, and strikes the second of the 'bells'. Here the flow of current is not interrupted by the movement of the striker, as it is in the previous case: so instead of getting thirty rings per second, you get a single 'ding' followed by a melodious 'dong' as the bell-push is released.

The switching on and off of circuits in this fashion has the makings of a data processing system, and the first of these appeared in the form of relay-operated automatic dialling systems for telephone exchanges. This mechanism (which was invented by an undertaker working in his spare time) gave rise in turn to calculators, and the demands of the Second World War — and the need to make quick calculations of bomb trajectories and so forth — led to a great acceleration in the development of the hardware to exploit the idea in practice.

The first of the large calculators, almost a direct forebear of the modern device with which we are all familiar, was designed by Howard H. Aitken of Harvard University and was built with the support of IBM. It was completed in 1944, and was designated the Automatic Sequence Controlled Calculator, with the uninspiring acronym ASCC as its working title. It was made up of a series of wheels for storing decimal numbers, seventy-two registers each holding twenty-four wheels (to hold twenty-three numbers together with a $+$ or $-$ sign). Each of the registers was connected to an adding mechanism which transferred a figure to another register, performing addition or subtraction. Multiplication and division were handled in units alongside, and there was a 'programmable' component in which a range of constants could be set by the operation of switches.

Relays were fitted to act as impulse transmitters, and the whole machine was extremely complicated. It was made up of three-quarters of a million components. But ASCC proved to be reliable, and worked successfully for over fifteen years. It was an *electrical* calculator, though, not an *electronic* one (see p. 104) and worked slowly by modern standards. Addition calculations took half a second, and complex division sums took ten or twelve seconds. But ASCC was a success, and it paved the way for the desk-top devices that were to follow in its footsteps.

What are transistors?

The transistor is a tiny sandwich of different kinds of doped silicon — a more complicated version of the diode we encountered on pp. 90-92. The sandwich can either be of a layer of negatively-doped silicon between two positively-doped layers, known as a P-N-P transistor, or it can be made with the negatively doped layers surrounding one that is positive, the N-P-N transistor. A change of electrical charge in the central region — the filler of the sandwich, known as the base — can bring about a change in the current flowing from the transistor. The device can also amplify current by as much as 100 times.

In a computer, the tiny trickle of current before amplification would correspond to the 'off' position of a 'switch' — the binary 0, whilst the much-increased amplified flow would be the 'on' mode, the binary 1.

The first investigations of solid components like this, as opposed to the glass valves of earlier years, stemmed from work on crystals like germanium which were known to be semi-conductors — i.e. they could carry current one way, but not the other. In this manner they were capable of rectifying an alternating current (q.v.). The earliest applications in the home were the crystal sets that were so popular after the Second World War. Every boy made one — it was a little radio with a small crystal of germanium which was held in a cup, against which a fine wire was placed, the so-called cat's whisker. By moving the 'whisker' around, the most responsive part of the crystal could be found and radio transmissions picked up loud and clear. I spent many hours hidden under the bed-sheets long after it was time to go to sleep as a boy, picking up the programmes from Brookman's Park, and hearing sneak previews of the first days of rock 'n' roll from the American Forces Network in Germany.

Before the war began, at the Bell Telephone Laboratories in the United States, a study of solid-state physics was launched and one of the first members of the team, William Shockley, predicted that: 'it should be possible to control the meager supply of movable electrons inside a semi-conductor by influencing them with an electric field imposed from outside.' The war years diverted attention to the more immediate problems of defence, and the semi-conductors found application in the detection of micro-waves from enemy radar transmitters. In particular, it was found that pure germanium crystals made an excellent detector.

When the research started up again, much attention was paid to Shockley's idea, namely to control the current flowing in a semi-conductor by an electrical charge outside it. Try as they might, there was no success. The effect seemed minimal. The silicon block with which they experimented was immersed in a solvent at one stage, in the hope that this would enable the electric charge outside to make a better contact, but to no avail.

Success came in a most unexpected way. The first time that an effect was demonstrated satisfactorily, it came about when a sample of germanium was substituted for the silicon of the earlier experiments. But then, when the effect was recorded, it was in the inverse direction to what had been predicted by Shockley's theories. Two research workers, Walter H Brattain and John Bardeen, tried a further experiment and succeeded in altering the rate of current flow from a semi-conductor by applying a control current through a contact — but here too, the effect was the opposite of what had been predicted. The result was the invention of the point-contact transistor, which functions quite differently from the externally-mediated model they began with.

From this, the more familiar junction transistor, made with specially doped layers of silicon, was developed. The development revolutionised the world of electronics, and changed the shape of the world for the public too (it is hard to find any corner of the world where a transistor radio is not a familiar sight). Yet it is worth bearing in mind that it was a discovery made by chance, and not because of a deliberate plan of action.

So how is a silicon chip different to a transistor?

The essential point is that the chip is covered with transistors, and with the wiring that runs between them. It is a question of scale. Obviously, one way to make a transistor is to take slices of doped silicon and join them together, with the appropriate wiring connections attached. That is how transistors were made originally.

But there is one important aspect to bear in mind. The functioning of these components depends on the nature of the layers, and not on how big the layers are. A tiny transistor works in the same way as a huge one. Though there are limits in the design of a miniaturised glass valve, for obvious reasons, they do not apply in the same way to a transistor. The smallest trace of the right material can act as well as a sizeable chunk of it — and it was in that simple realisation that the dawn of the micro-chip arose.

Instead of assembling transistors piece by piece, an entire circuit was built up on a disc of silicon. As the tiny layers were carefully placed in position, the p- and n- type materials were built up to form the layers we would recognise as being the transistor components, fine slivers of conductor were laid down, carrying the current from one region of the chip to another, and in this way a whole complex array of electronic units was assembled, systematically, in one single component.

The first of these was made in 1970 by Texas Instruments for use in defence electronic systems and also in space-craft, where miniaturisation was at a premium. The truly awe-inspiring nature of these components is their diminutive size. Many of them vie with bacteria for smallness. How is it done? That is often asked — and the answer is that we resort to photography to do it. The template for a specific process is cut out and photographically projected onto the chip under construction. In the same way that a fine meshwork of silver lines would appear in a photographic negative, if that was how the image had been recorded at that place on the film, a thin array of conductors — or any other kind of component — could be produced on the surface of a chip by photographic means.

The research I have most recently seen in operation suggests that the final limits will be to produce transistors some two or three thousandths of a millimetre in size (about as big as a *Staphylococcus* bacterium) and the fine conductors can be no more than 0.1μm wide — i.e. one ten-thousandth of a millimetre.

That is fine enough to pack a quarter of a million of them inside a human hair-shaft. Each of the microscopic switching sites in the chip itself is usually known as a gate (the analogy is a good one; open and shut the gate and the

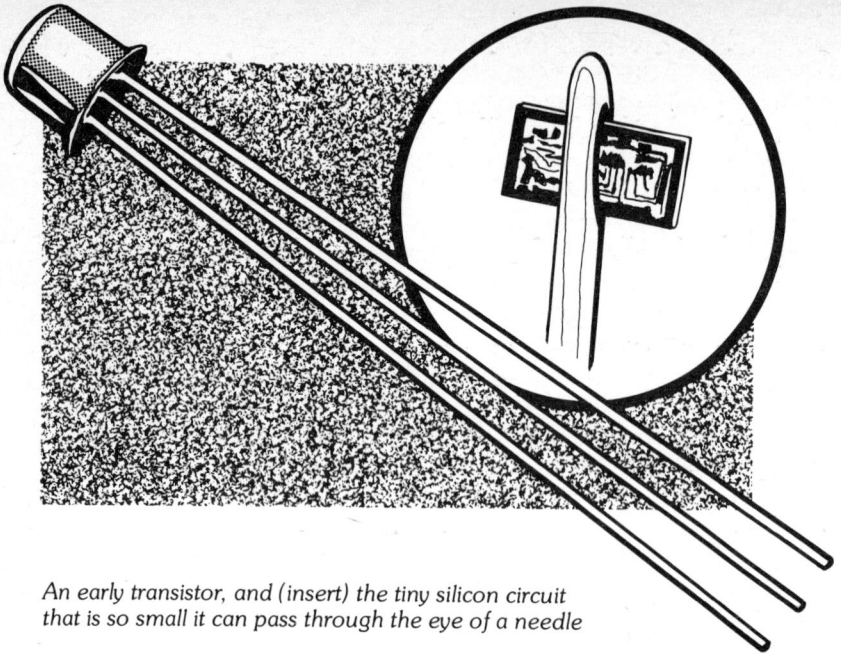

An early transistor, and (insert) the tiny silicon circuit that is so small it can pass through the eye of a needle

'switch' is on or off, corresponding to the 1 and 0 of the binary ASCII code), and the current aim is to pack 2.5×10^7 gates into a square centimetre (that is twenty-five million, if you prefer the long-hand version).

The trend towards miniaturisation means that by the time we have reached that stage, you would have the calculating power of the original ENIAC in an area no bigger that a ten-thousandth of a square centimetre, and that in less than four decades. At the moment the density is around 200,000 gates per square centimetre, so the greatest number of ENIACS you would find in that square centimetre is a mere ten. Every five years since the 1950s the number of components that can fit into a given area of a silicon chip has increased tenfold. It has been a revolution in technology which probably matches something like the discovery of fire, or the invention of the wheel.

What is the point of miniaturisation?

The main aim is simply driven by the fun of being first, of setting new limits, and wanting to make scientific news. The field leaders know each other, they watch each other's laboratories like hawks, and each is keen to be the first to break new ground and make a little history for themselves. The security controls at computer research establishments are astonishingly strict. So are the levels of cleanliness that have to be observed. But there are great similarities between the different centres, imposed by the nature of the exercise. Many of those that I have visited have presented one with the most exciting insights: but of course, they all guard secrets from each other madly and so there is little I can reveal here. . . .

Even though personal excitement and the nature of the challenge are certainly the principal motivating forces at work, there are practical considerations too. One factor is the sheer compactness, of course: the fact that a calculator chip can be installed in a wristwatch or that a computer can go into your coat pocket (or a space-craft) is a clear advance.

A third factor is that of economy. Miniaturised modules consume minute amounts of raw materials, and at a time when rare elements are being hard-pressed and demand would soon outstrip supply if earlier technologies were applied, the sheer savings in raw material consumption, and raw material cost, are vital.

Fourth is the fact that small units consume smaller amounts of electricity. The computers of the 1950s were attached to a heavy fuel bill, whilst modern portable units can function on batteries designed originally for hearing-aids. Electrical power demands are actually a *constraint* in producing microchips, because the heat generated has to be dissipated.

Fifth is the fact that electricity does have a finite speed, so the shorter the distance a signal has to travel, the sooner it is transmitted from source to destination. Smaller systems work faster, therefore.

We will continue to see a race towards smaller and smaller units. They all combine to produce a sense of competition and impetus between the pioneering companies which it would be hard to equal anywhere else.

Against this, however, one has to set the limiting factor of human size. No person could possibly handle chips as tiny as these and make connections to other modules. Even transistors once needed to be mounted in a holder to facilitate connection. So these microscopic chips are themselves contained in components that are thousands of times bigger, just to ensure that you do not lose your vastly powerful computer in the cuffs of your shirt, or drop it between the floorboards.

Are digital recordings successful?

Yes, they are, and indeed the concept of the digital transmission of any signal — from a commercial sound recording or any other source — confers clear benefits over many of the alternatives. The standard means of making a sound recording was to use the wave-form itself transferred either to a plastic vinyl disc, in which case the sound was represented by an undulating groove which was the same shape as the sound wave it represented; or a magnetic recording compound, in which case the sound was represented by variations in the magnetisation of the surface. Both of these were analog recordings, since the impulses were analogous to the original signal.

In the case of digitised information, the wave-form is translated into a series of precisely defined data which itself defines the way the sound-wave was generated. That data was subsequently encoded in digital form.

And this is where the benefit becomes apparent. Whereas the signal, i.e. the original wave-form, can be degraded with time and with poor electronic handling, and can be swamped to a greater or lesser extent by background sounds or by electrical interference, the digital version is entirely immune to such noise. This encoded version is represented either by the presence or absence of a signal, by 1 or by 0, and nothing else. So if the signal is indistinctly transmitted in some way there is no effect on the quality of the sound that results. All the receiver has to do is recognise whether the signal is a 1 or a 0, just that. It is the difference between trying to memorise the objects around you in a room on the one hand (the analog version) or simply having to detect whether the light in the room is on, or whether the room itself is in darkness (the digital equivalent). It is a far easier task of discrimination, and is carried out unequivocally. It is the difference between trying to hear an indistinct telephone call, swamped with echoes and line noise on the one hand, or taking down a message by morse on the other. The morse (which is here nearer to the digital model) will give the same message whether the sound is high or low, loud or soft. As long as you can hear the presence or absence of the signal you can interpret the transmission perfectly. But even the clearest telephone line can make it hard to distinguish between someone saying 'F' and somebody else saying 'S'.

Digital signals can suffer a great deal of attenuation, or weakening, and a great deal of interference too, before they become indistinct. Only when the signal vanishes altogether does the message fail to get through. For that reason the digital transmission of a piece of recorded music down the telephone line becomes feasible, given enough time, and the transfer of a studio recording to disc is more reliable when the signal is digitalised.

The practical limitation centres on the ability of the digitising process to translate the music into data with sufficient accuracy, or resolution, to become a faithful rendition of the original. These constraints mean that the amplitude resolution (i.e. the number of different levels of amplitude that can be accommodated) must be 2^{16} or 65,536, and that the number of discrete data sampled per second must be 50,000. The number of bits of data that are generated per second if those limits are met must be $16 \times 50,000 = 800,000$ bits.

The range of sound levels handled should be 96 dB, and since the highest sound frequency that can be heard by the healthy child is up to 20,000 Hz (i.e. 20,000 vibrations per second) it follows that a range of 0-20,000 Hz will accommodate the maximum hearing range of the human ear.

Naturally, the digital recording is not the same as the analog one and it cannot convey as much accuracy in theory. Sound waves are smoothly modulated, whilst the digital version is broken up into a series of sharp steps. The theory breaks down because of the difficulty of actually transferring the

100

analog reception of sound waves into a successful form — the noise, scatter and interference see to that — and in any case the digital system outlined above, even if it is not as good as the original sound, is still much clearer to the human ear. We do not have a frequency range greater than 50-17,000 Hz as adults, and can certainly not perceive more than 50,000 changes in waveform per second! The digital record, then, is better than the human ear, even if not as good as nature.

Digital discs for the enthusiast are made up of small discrete pits that are etched into the surface of a virtually-indestructible disc that looks rather like an L.P. These are read by means of a laser which scans the surface, and the resulting digital output is amplified and converted back into sound waves, thus providing the end-product. This is an extremely condensed form of digital information, and some variation on this theme would provide an efficient way of supplying input for domestic computers.

A video-disc, which is the ultimate in solid-state data storage available for everyday use, has a capacity for storing over one thousand million bytes of information in more than 50,000 frames, any one of which can be selected and displayed within seconds. It may be that this idea will be exploited in the future as a means of providing take-away software for the home micro user.

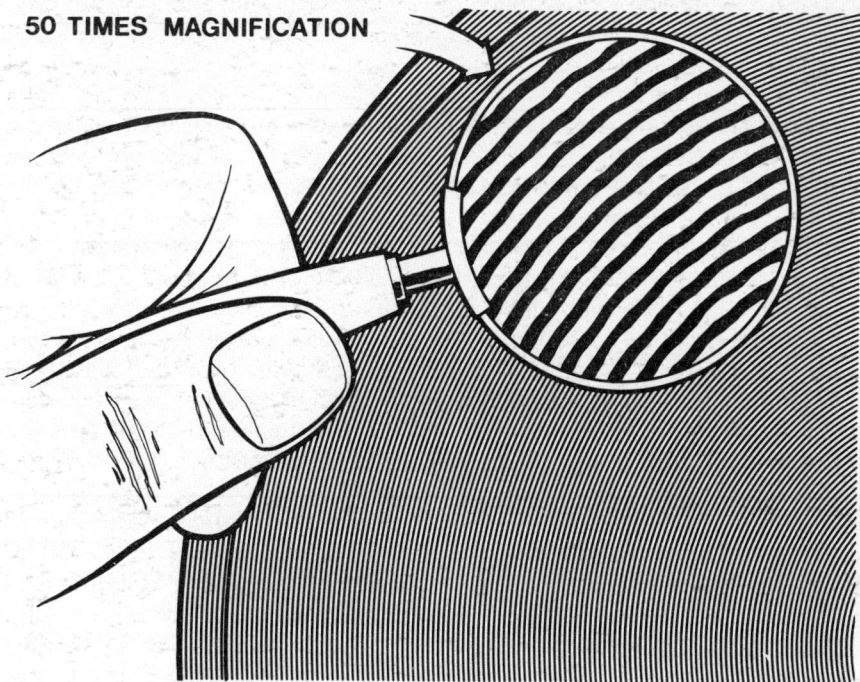

50 TIMES MAGNIFICATION

Surface of L.P.

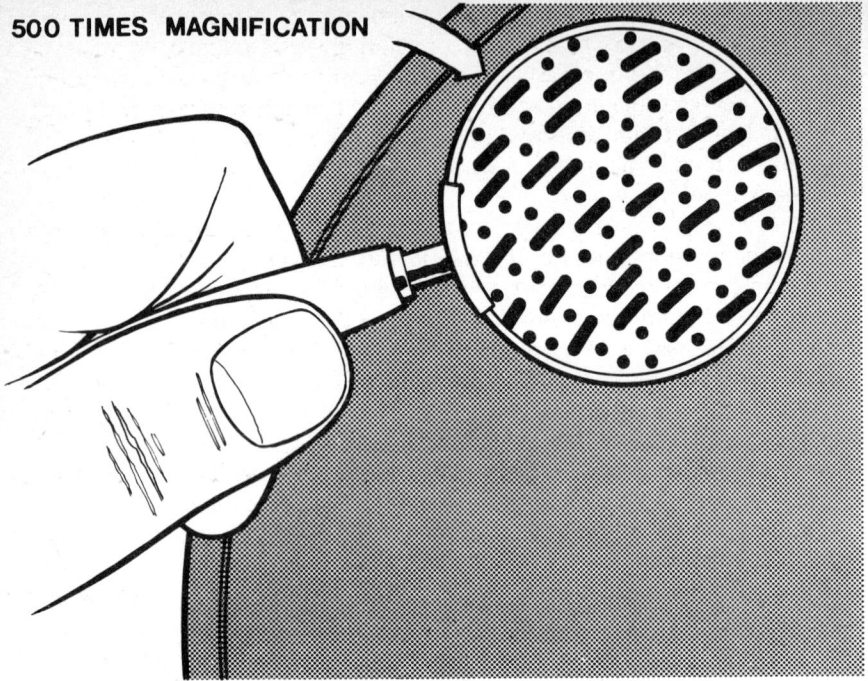

500 TIMES MAGNIFICATION

Surface of compact disc

What about optical transmission?

This is a method of handling data that will become of great importance within a few years. In the past we have transmitted data through wires or radio signals. The quality of data that can be transmitted depend upon the wavelength of the carrier. A long-wave transmission (such as Radio Four, 1500 metres) has a wavelength that is, as it says, almost a mile. The quality of sound that can be transmitted is therefore poor, and any attempt at 'hi-fi' impossible. Medium-wave transmissions are shorter (like the eighth-of-a-mile wavelength of Radio Luxemburg, 208 metres). VHF or FM transmissions have a much shorter wavelength than even the older 'short-wave' (typically 50 metres); in this case we are now down to around a metre or two. So more information can be transmitted, and the sound quality is very much better than in the case of the radio transmissions of an earlier era.

The rationale behind the use of wavelengths of light is easily appreciated, once this sense of values for radio wavelengths has been understood. The wavelength of a light ray is less than one-thousandth of a millimetre. So we are speaking here of a transmission medium which is not just a dozen times better than radio waves, but millions of times better. Some comparison can

102

be made between the carrying of simultaneous transmissions of human speech down a wire, in which case the total number you could carry would be around 250, and the number you could theoretically carry via a laser beam, which has been calculated to be 100,000 million, an improvement of virtually a billion. The fact that present-day systems are one thousand times worse than that potential still means they are a million times more effective than what we had before.

Of those figures, few mean much in conceptual terms. The essential bed-rock of the argument does not rely on mathematical juggling: it is plain that a light beam can carry information of an inordinately complicated form, and is an inconceivable improvement on a radio system. So that is the answer to the *why* of fibre optics.

The *how* is based on the fact that a glass rod can carry a beam of light along its length. There is a phenomenon known as total internal reflection, which means that if light travelling along a rod of glass is moving towards the edge of the rod, it cannot escape. Instead it is reflected back, towards the centre of the structure. It is a little like marbles shot down a drain-pipe. All the light comes out at the end (apart from any fraction which is reflected by dust or bubbles in the glass).

Fibre optics units are made by drawing out rods until they are exceedingly fine, like hairs. If the ends are made perfectly flat, then light shone in at one end will emerge with virtually no loss at the other. More to the point, if a bundle of parallel glass fibres is bound together, an image presented to one end will be seen by an observer at the other, in original form. This application has been of the greatest use in endoscopes, which can inspect hidden parts of the body. There is no need for lenses and prisms in this system, the light follows the fibres which can be bent as flexibly as the threads of a glass-fibre mat.

As for the *when* aspect, it has all happened in recent years because of the development of the laser. Radio waves could be made of a specified wavelength, and the laser produces a beam of coherent light, in which all the light is of the same wavelength, and all the separate wave-fronts are exactly in step with each other. The result is that we have a new and exciting method of data transmission. By turning the laser beam on and off, we can code for the 0s and 1s of the binary code, and in this way send data in digital form and under very crowded conditions. Tests on a system that is going to run between New York City and Washington D.C., for instance, show that a single bundle of fibres no bigger than your middle finger could carry more than 200,000 phone conversations at one time.

In the same way, it is impossible for a metallic wire to carry the 1½ million impulses per second that would code for a colour television picture. But the same number of pulses transmitted through a single glass fibre system would be no problem. And so direct transmission of television signals becomes feasible.

At present there are some optical transmission systems in operation. One early example for telephone communication was installed between the Isle of Wight and the mainland in 1982, and a more complex network was built in Biarritz, on the Atlantic coast of France, providing 1500 subscribers with videophones, videotext and television channels. A new cable network has been completed between Boston and Washington, on the American east coast, Japan is planning a nationwide system to link every major town, and there are plans for a trans-Atlantic subterranean optical fibre link connecting London and New York City.

The length of the optical fibres is the problem, and joining one section to another is not easy. Now current technology makes it realistic to transmit data for about ten miles before it is 'boosted' for the next segment of its journey. And since the information is being sent in digital form, there are only those 1s and 0s to bother with. Signal deterioration is a thing of the past, and you can end up with a message as loud and as clear as the one you began with thousands of miles away.

What is the difference between 'electronic' and 'electric'?

It is not, as some think, that the former word is merely an up-dated and more trendy version of the latter. The essential difference is that *electronic devices* involve *amplification*: they contain components that can change the virtual absence of current (corresponding to the 0 in the binary code) to the presence of current (corresponding to 1). Units which carry electric current only if it travels in one direction are known as rectifiers; and combinations of this kind of component enable us to build up arrays of switches and amplifiers which allow current to flow in specific pathways whilst diverting it from others. In this way, the complex system of 0s and 1s which embody the data you wish to feed in, is built up.

7 Philosophy and the Future

Have we got micro-computers out of proportion?

Certainly we have, and there is an interesting historical perspective that you might like to consider. A hundred years ago and more, many families had a microscope. The craze arose in the mid-nineteenth century, when lenses were produced of such quality that they enabled the user to see as much as is theoretically possible with an optical microscope. The manufacturers were no fools, and went on making microscopes festooned with facilities that in many cases were entirely unnecessary. There are some that are so elaborate that they are almost impossible to use, so cluttered are they with these superfluous accessories.

The fact is that microscopes, at that time, were just a fashionable craze, in just the same way that computers are now. People bought them not because they actually *needed* them, or because they were necessary, but because they had the latest gadget, the up-to-date facility, and looked acceptable in that materialistic age. It was a question of keeping up with one's acquaintances, and following the fashion, rather like today's status race with new cars which are last year's models with the latest drag-reducing spoiler or the latest go-faster stripe down one side.

The important thing to bear in mind is that the value of a microscope (like that of a computer) is what it can show us about our world, and how it can help us. The insight we gained into bacteria, hygiene and so forth made the microscope and what I have called 'microscopic consciousness' very useful — but there was no need for everybody to buy the latest type. Nowadays hardly anybody has one, and we are not exactly consumed with epidemics as a result.

Students of nonscience will know that I regard the study of the changes in scientific crazes as a discipline of its own, called *fashionism*. It explains the way that topics like cholesterol and white sugar disappear whilst new vogues (including fibre and micro-computers) become the new topic for attention.

But you might well ask why the computer craze is so much bigger than many of the others. We have had past surges of interest in cameras, in hi-fi, and now in home computers; but the computer craze surpasses all the others. The reason is, I believe, that computers throw some different light on reality — on how we perceive ourselves, and how we tinker with our view of what is truth. Around ten years before the present, there was an upsurge in paranormal studies: people were seeing with their fingers and toes, communicating via the absent, even the dead, and bending spoons and forks without so much as a breath to do the damage. Ten years before that, it was psychogenic drugs, from marijuana to lysergic acid (more recent years have been filled in with cocaine). It is as though human beings have a strong desire to bend and tinker with reality, to create new levels of consciousness. That is the great extra dimension that computers have over cameras and hi-fi sets — they can be made to carry out what seem to be strange mental activities. The micro-computer can give a taste of out-of-the-ordinary psychological experiences.

I doubt whether any of what computers do can be construed as 'intelligence' (a matter I'll return to on p. 110) but that is not the point. Users imagine they are dicing with amazing, mind-boggling ideas and in that sense the micro is a successor to the mind-bending manipulators (both human and biochemical) of earlier decades. That may well be why the microscope, a hundred years ago, was such a clear parallel to today's home computer. Apart from being a glittering, impressive, complex gadget, the microscopes of the Victorian era showed forms of life and aspects of existence that were not otherwise available for scrutiny.

The lesson is that mankind loves toys to play with, no matter at what age we may be. And when the toy seeks to show something mystical, metaphysical or mind-boggling, then it is bound to be a sure-fire success. (It takes a human to work out something like that incidentally — not a computer.)

A second, and perhaps more salutary, conclusion is that you do not need to be *au fait* with the operation of computers to exist comfortably in an environment in which they feature prominently. There is a need for us all to be computer-*aware*, so that we are not intimidated by the machines themselves, but you do not need to know how to program to obtain money from a cash-point, any more than you need to know how to use a microscope before you can clean your teeth. My view is that there will be a large number of terminals as part of our daily lives in a few decades, yet — surprising as it may seem now — very few people will wish or need to know anything at all about programming.

Will home computers do away with going to work?

Many people have thought so, but the facts do not — so far — bear them out. One US company set up a group of fifty 'alternate site workers', as they were called, each with a terminal at home, obviating any need to go to work. The novelty soon wore off, as the individuals reported feeling lost, lonely, isolated — and asked for a chance to get together again.

A word-processing company near Minneapolis reportedly reached the conclusion that people needed people. They began to arrange meetings and lunches in the office every week at least. The head of the firm emphasised that they realised how few of their workers were really hermits by nature; we need to meet to get the creative juices flowing, he said. This may be another case of society ignoring the social demands of being human. In that sense, the simplistic answers of the computer buff may not meet the real demands of real people. Survey data seem to confirm this. One report prepared for *Time* magazine in 1982 showed that three-quarters of the US population considered that the computer revolution would enable people to work at home, rather than in an office or factory with their fellow. But less than a third of the respondents said they would like to do so themselves.

We have often neglected the need of human beings to act through societies and through group hierarchies. People derive a sense of security from belonging in a societal structure, and the isolation of being marooned at home with a terminal would take away much of the chance for human interrelation and interaction that we need to become entire adults.

To two categories of people this does not apply. Rather, the converse is the rule. These are the handicapped, and the bed-bound victims of debilitating disease. Here the home-based terminal can be the key to work which would otherwise be unavailable. Severely handicapped people can communicate, study and work from their homes, through the use of a computer. At least one crippled poliomyelitis victim now works from his chair as a full-time programmer, after a lifetime of isolation. For people like that, the home terminal computer can be a godsend.

But it is not merely the shedding of 25,000 jobs in the Department of Health and Social Security which has caused a minor rebellion against the decision to computerise the State benefits system. People are also pointing out that the storing of such information in a central data-bank gives access to personal details in a form that any clerk can summon in an instant, and which could be broken into by hackers. Here too, the working clerk seems to be preferred to an all-knowing, non-thinking memory.

Are computers bad for you?

Husbands who terrorise their children or abandon their wives to the demon screen are a menace and should be . . . well, discouraged. The screens themselves have been associated with eye-strain. But the only actual health hazard I have come across was a claim by a Dr Eliot from Omaha, Nebraska, who said that children playing *Donkey Kong* and *Pac-man* became so wound up emotionally that they developed hypertension. He said that he had treated some children as young as fourteen for their blood pressure, and was quoted as saying: 'I have some lads who will be on anti-blood pressure pills for the rest of their lives.' That may well be a warning to a parent who wants a good reason to step in and prevent an addictive excess of computer-mania. But I am bound to add that I'm none too sure whether that is a genuine quote. Have you ever heard a doctor from the state of Nebraska calling a lad a 'lad'?

Is there a future for electronic money?

It is hard to see that money will vanish altogether. For purchases of small items, or taxi-fares, or for the money-in-the-hand transactions that are a mainstay of personal business in every country, it is hard to see that the people would willingly accept a micro-chip that read all, calculated all, and — more to the point — recorded all. If electronic money were to become universal, then you could argue that every transaction would be so clearly documented that there would be no confusion, no overcharging, and no doubt about liability.

Against that would be the argument of those who insist that such matters are a personal concern, allied with people who would (rightly) point out that any system of data control involving more than a few tens of thousands of data is bound to have mistakes in it. In that sense, there would be as much argument over money in a completely automated era as there is now.

There are already some benefits through the use of electronic cash systems, of which the most familiar must surely be the cash-point facility, the computer terminal which accepts a card with a magnetic message imprinted on the back. The message is not always where you expect it to be, though. For instance in the first of the cash-dispenser cards, there was a broad brown magnetic stripe, with a narrower green arrow alongside it, indicating which way the card was meant to be inserted into the machine. The encoded information was not situated in the stripe at all, but in the arrow, as a means of discouraging tampering.

Using such cards it is now possible to call up your current balance (unless the phone lines are closed or the computer unit is on holiday, so they are often useless at weekends), order a statement or a cheque-book, or withdraw cash in the form of £5 or £10 notes on demand. The benefits are obvious. The disadvantages are less so:

1. These machines manage, through some kind of electronic telepathy it seems, to withhold money from you through a machine disfunction only at the times when your need is most urgent;

2. The queues that form seem longer than ever before, only they are now outside in the freezing rain rather than inside in a nice warm bank (indeed it pays to glance into the building before using an exterior terminal, as the tills may well be completely empty, and ready to deal with you quicker than the terminal);

3. Errors are hard to challenge. Many of these terminals now give an option 'DO YOU WISH FOR A RECEIPT?' and many users press the 'NO' button to save time. That is bad practice, as it means that you have undertaken a transaction and indicated to the computer's memory your lack of interest in keeping a record of the fact. The opportunity to demonstrate that you drew out £5,

when £55 has been debited (should that occur) vanishes when there is no documentation to prove otherwise.

In addition, the debiting of sums when you did not actually use your card, but through the interference of someone else's data in your own store in the computer memory, would be hard to challenge in either event. Banks have tended to become more insistent on their own righteousness in recent years, issuing rules that state that the drawer of a cheque is liable for any inaccuracies it might contain (which means that a forger is your responsibility, not theirs) and that their own rules transcend, to cite one actual example, any laws or statutes to the contrary. Quite what happens when a bank customer challenges an erroneous print-out I hate to think, and would be glad to know about if such an event should occur to anyone reading these words.

But the cards now in use are capable of performing more tasks than at present they do. Credit cards in France are commonly slid through a reader which automatically reads the data encoded in them, and many times I have had to explain that back home in England we still put them into a machine with a handle, and print out the characters that are embossed on the card through carbon paper. French shop assistants give a slightly condescending smile at this juncture, and settle down to copy the words out laboriously when a card has just slid into their automatic reader, and then slid out again without triggering the essential mechanism.

France was actually the first country to take the next step after that, with the issue of pioneering 'smart cards' in 1982. They agreed to issue 20,000 cards by CII-Honeywell Bull in the town of Blois, 50,000 Phillips cards in Caen, and a further 50,000 cards made by Flonic-Schlumberger in Lyon. 200-250 terminals were set up in those city's shops and restaurants to act as payment points. The sums due at the end of each transaction were automatically debited to the card-holder's bank account without any need to copy out details, or even to print out the identification on the card itself.

A smart-card shipping experiment, which was claimed to pave the way for all of us in the future, was first planned by Honeywell Bull for Vélizy, a suburb of Paris. There a sample of 2,500 homes were linked to a videotext information network, and of those, 700 were provided with terminals with direct access to the stores' supplies. House-bound shopping could be done automatically, the goods selected, paid for electronically by direct debit from the bank, and the items themselves turned up by special delivery.

The plans for America's first experiments were centred on Fargo, North Dakota and Minneapolis-St Paul, and similar trials are under way in Britain too.

Obviously there are benefits in this concept. There is no need to travel to the store, to write cheques, or to stick to opening hours. But here we are faced with the social consequences of remote-control shopping. The experience of going round to the store and inspecting goods is for many people an important item of their daily routine, and a means of contact and refreshment. There is no great benefit in driving people into a state where so many of life's daily activities are subjugated to machinery that there is little to do but watch TV all the time. So let us keep both sides in perspective. With care, we could make a marvellous future for ourselves with the best of all worlds.

However, there are reports from France that official sources were using the memory of the shopping systems to check up on who had purchased what. This is a reminder of the invasive nature of 'official surveillance' which could allow government departments to check on private transactions and to do so invisibly. So the brave new world of tomorrow will need careful planning, or it might invade our private lives.

How do you evaluate artificial intelligence?

Frankly, I question its relationship to real intelligence. Artificial intelligence research (AI) has been going on for decades. Indeed some research centres were fancifully rumoured to have stopped their research because of fears that it might turn against them!

This is a vast and complex area of philosophy into which we cannot enter here, at least in detail. In my view the problem lies in the nature of perception. Human beings do not perceive in the way machines do. I believe that we make selective decisions based on codes of criteria that are partly innate, partly taught as a necessary part of our upbringing, and partly acquired. Fashion, expediency, notions of prestige and many others are part of that. We do not store up digitised quanta of knowledge like a computer, ours rests in a dichotomous tree of understanding, each layer of which selects for the next.

We can make machines that detect stimuli and respond to them, computers that store data, memories that recall vast columns of figures. All of them can out-perform a human, as can a pile of books, a racehorse, or a pair of nail-clippers. Computers can be made to synthesise aspects of human behaviour, like walking or seeing, talking or listening. In just the same way a film can imitate love, a bunch of plastic flowers ape a vase of fresh-cut blooms.

Yet these are not human manifestations, only travesties of small portions of them. Living systems are able to derive knowledge in so many ways, to seek new avenues of information if conventional ones dry up, to find new means of interpreting facts, figures, ideas and even to follow the occasional intuitive hunch.

There is a majesty about living systems which the essential crudity of a computer cannot match. Within a single living cell — and you are made of billions — are regulatory and control mechanisms, systems of communication and so much more that we cannot begin to fathom for ourselves. I have suggested in this book that there is a current craze for home computers which will settle into some kind of perspective in due course and that, I am sure, is likely to be the case. Yet computers and control systems powering robots, cash-flow and documentation of so many kinds will revolutionise our world, and offer a considerable possibility to make tomorrow a more balanced, more democratic, and more open kind of society.

But that does not make them threats to the wisdom of men and women. Artificial intelligence strikes me as being more artificial than intelligent. Machines are different to humans, not rivals.

And that is what makes them so intriguing.

Index